It's been 120 days since the start of our adventure. Today I ask myself, "Is this nonsense? Why have we suffered freezing temperatures, hunger, thirst? Why have we battled with muddy, rocky, and sandy roads? Why are we risking our lives?

# Books by Carlos A. Caggiani

1998
*Deshojando Recuerdos*


2002
*Un Nuevo Martín Fierro*


2009
*Huellas y Horizontes:*
*26 Países en una Motocicleta*

*Ingeniería de una Estafa*

# Tracks and Horizons

## 26 Countries on a Motorcycle

Carlos A. Caggiani

# Tracks and Horizons
© 2010 Carlos A. Caggiani

Cover artwork and English translation by Ed Caggiani.

First edition: September 2010
ISBN: 14-5378-537-X
EAN-13: 9781453785379


www.TracksAndHorizons.com

Printed in the United States of America
CreateSpace.com

www.CarlosCaggiani.com

# Acknowledgements

To my son Ed, who besides designing the cover artwork and translating this book into English, also made the publishing possible.

To my loving wife Piedad, with whom I share the final years of my life. You keep the child in me alive.

To my grandchildren Nicholas, Isabella, Juan Camilo, and Mateo, who are the light in my eyes.

To all the people I mention in this book and those I have had the opportunity to share my adventure with.

# Cities

Rio de Janeiro, Brazil
Rivera, Uruguay
Minas de Corrales, Uruguay
Tacuarembó, Uruguay
Montevideo, Uruguay
Colonia, Uruguay
Buenos Aires, Argentina
Termas de Rio Hondo, Argentina
Córdoba, Argentina
Tucumán, Argentina
Humahuaca, Argentina
La Quiaca, Argentina
Villazón, Bolivia
Potosí, Bolivia
La Paz, Bolivia
Puno, Peru
Arequipa, Peru
Lima, Peru
Chimbote, Peru
Trujillo, Peru
Chiclayo, Peru
Piura, Peru
Tumbes, Peru
Desaguaderos, Ecuador
Port Bolivar, Ecuador
Guayaquil, Ecuador
Quito, Ecuador
Cali, Colombia
Buenaventura, Colombia
Panama City, Panama
San Jose, Costa Rica
Managua, Nicaragua
Tegucigalpa, Honduras
San Salvador, El Salvador
Guatemala City, Guatemala
Tapachula, Mexico
Tuxtla Gutiérrez, Mexico
Veracruz, Mexico
Mexico City, Mexico
Guadalajara, Mexico
Hermosillo, Mexico
Tijuana, Mexico
Los Angeles, USA

Seal Beach, USA
Newport Beach, USA
Santa Ana, USA
Long Beach, USA
San Francisco, USA
Reno, USA
Denver, USA
New York City, USA
Newark, USA
Jersey City, USA
St. John's, Canada
Dublin, Ireland
Liverpool, England
Manchester, England
Birmingham, England
London, England
Ramsgate, England
Dover, England
Calais, France
Paris, France
Brussels, Belgium
Amsterdam, Netherlands
Aachen, Germany
Bonn, Germany
Frankfurt, Germany
Berne, Switzerland
Turin, Italy
Genoa, Italy
Pisa, Italy
Florence, Italy
Arezzo, Italy
Perugia, Italy
Rome, Italy
Civitavecchia, Italy
Piombino, Italy
Livorno, Italy
Nice, France
Toulon, France
Marseilles, France
Badalona, Spain
Barcelona, Spain
Lisbon, Portugal
Montevideo, Uruguay

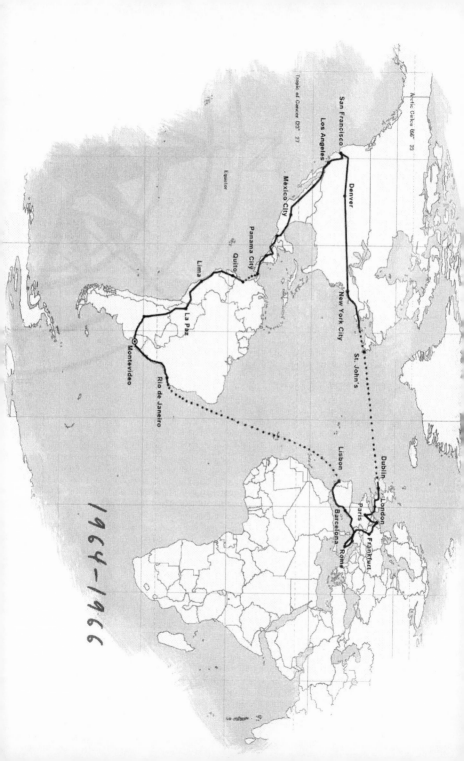

# Table of Contents

# Foreword

Growing up, I remember being amazed by the stories of my father's youthful adventures. It was hard to believe the man in those stories was the same man who taught me my first guitar chord, showed me how to properly compose a photograph, and opened my eyes to the wonders of art and creativity.

His stories always came in non-chronological bits and pieces, forcing me to reconstruct his two-year motorcycle journey in my mind over the span of many years. It wasn't until he wrote the original Spanish version of this book, *Huellas y Horizontes*, in 2009 that I was able to put the entire picture together. What I discovered was that his story was more important than I had imagined. His experiences between 1964 and 1966 affected him greatly and helped make him the man he is today – and the one who taught me all those things for which I've been grateful.

When he decided he wanted to translate *Huellas y Horizontes* into English, I knew I had to be a part of it. Sample translations from a few services I researched just did not feel right to me. They did a fine job translating the words, but in many cases lost the passion and emotion in his writing. So I volunteered to work on the translation myself. I was hesitant at first since I'm not a professional writer or translator. But I felt I would be the only one who could be true to my father's voice.

It's been nearly two years since I read his first draft and began the translation. This project has become an amazing journey, bringing me closer to my father. It helped me further see him as a man with principles and honor, a man who has known suffering and has triumphed over adversity. Through this book, he has taught me life lessons all over again.

Even though I had already read his book, I would often get caught up in it all over again during my translation, and I'd have to force myself to keep going. There were many times when I'd be typing through moist eyes as I'd imagine my father saying the words he'd written.

When my mother died in 1999, I saw a pain in my father's eyes I had never seen before. It was a sad time, but seeing the love my father had for my mother affected me deeply. His outward defenses were lowered and he showed us his true, bare self… emotional, caring, and loving.

I now understand why he is who he is. He is a man shaped by experience, both good and bad. He is a writer, artist, musician, mentor, and role model. He's a business-man, entrepreneur, and engineer. But to me, most importantly, he is my father.

*Ed Caggiani*
*September 2010*

# Prologue

Many years have passed. Memories begin to unravel in my mind and I ask myself if any of the tracks I have laid down over the years will remain when the end draws near. I have worn grooves that will undoubtedly be covered by the relentless winds of time.

They say that a real man is one who has had children, written a book, and planted a tree. I've had children, written two books, but have never planted a tree, nor do I have any intention of doing so, for even though I enjoy beautiful gardens, I abhor gardening. I have dedicated a good part of my life to literature and the admiration of writers who are capable of awakening the imagination with their subtleties. Writing about myself is not easy, and my intention in doing so is to one day allow my grandchildren and my great grandchildren to understand the reasons behind the decisions I've made, and to help them realize there's always a motivation behind even the most innocent action.

Frank McCourt, the Irish-American teacher and Pulitzer-Prize winning author, required that his students write about themselves, yet he was hesitant in chronicling his own life. When he finally decided to write *Angela's Ashes*, he left an extraordinary legacy that highlighted the tracks of his life, good and bad.

That's what this is all about… transcribing our memories before we part this world. It's about leaving an imprint in the ground that is hard to erase. Every human being has his own life story, and each story, whether entertaining or not, should be planted like a family tree in the garden of our successors. What better knowledge can we impart to future generations?

Life passes quickly and our tracks get filled in by time. The written word remains as a legacy that helps our memories endure. More significantly, it helps future readers understand the most important question of all... why?

# 1.

# Looking for answers

Long after my two-year motorcycle adventure, after living many years in the United States, I returned to my birthplace, Montevideo, Uruguay. It was a changed place. It's not as if time stood still; it's as if the memories I had of the place had transformed. I looked upon the streets of my birth city and I hardly recognized them. I stumbled on potholes and got wet from the moisture trapped under the loose cobblestones of the sidewalks from my childhood. The ancient roots of the trees that provided me with welcome shade in my youth have, with the passage of time and their inevitable growth, entrusted themselves with the cracking and lifting of the sidewalks I've walked on so many times.

The colonial buildings of 18 De Julio (Main Street) changed from the familiar clear colors to an aged flat grey matte, accentuating their total lack of maintenance. The late model Mercedes Benz taxis have been replaced by small economic cars with dangerous glass security partitions, and the modern silent trolleys of my youth have become a part of history.

I walked tirelessly trying to find at least a semblance of what I left behind, until I realized it no longer existed. I travelled Centenario Avenue from Pueblito Nuevo to the stadium. I recalled making this trip with my father almost every weekend that Nacional, our favorite soccer team, would play. I could almost hear my dad yelling a warning not to cross the street alone, *"Carlitos... no cruces la calle solo... esperá... dame la mano!"*

The grass on the central gardens looked dry, and the little reddish rocks that circled them were no longer there. The café on Centenario and Agaces, where my father was once a nighttime regular in the smoke-and-alcohol-filled card games, had also disappeared.

I stood in the doorway of a garage and thought how out of place it seemed in a neighborhood where no one had a car. I heard the echo that remained in my mind of that 16th of July in 1950 when Uruguay won the World Cup against the seemingly invincible Brazil. I relived the many championships of the Munar Futbol Club and the parties we had in my old garage that was not only part of my home, but also the team's headquarters.

In my anxious search I reached Propios Street. The sculpture studio of Don Vero, where I learned so much, was also missing. On the corner of Montecaseros and Echandía, they tore down my Grandmother Doña Clara's old house and started constructing an apartment building, only to leave it an unfinished reminder of what could have been. I found it strange that the Café de La Via was still there, a bit older but with a new name.

From the Port of Montevideo to Carrasco, I travelled La Rambla and I remembered cruising with my mascot Chico, a capuchin monkey my friend Melo brought back from Brazil who became my motorcycle riding companion. Chico was well known in Montevideo, and he certainly facilitated my interactions with the ladies. In winter, Chico would wear a leather jacket and a sweater with the initials CH. He would sit on the gas tank of my bike and grab the handlebars with his little furry hands, enjoying the speed. He was my mascot and great companion. I remembered the pain I felt the day I received a letter at the Uruguayan consulate in Paris informing me of his death after an illness.

I thought about my youth, my studies, my loves, my invention of the S.U.N. personal water heater, motorcycles, races, trips to Brazil and Argentina, my nearly two-year motorcycle trip around the world and my return, and finally my departure for the United States in search of opportunities.

Observing a young boy eating food from a garbage can right in front of me, as if it was the most natural thing in the world, was a shocking sight. This sadly explained the statue in front of Independence Square of a child rummaging through the trash.

I recalled walking into the "Old City" when I was working on my first patent. I remembered the old patent office, the cobbled streets and my endless walks. In 1963, neither the child nor the statue of his hunger existed.

The idea of the S.U.N. heater was born one day when I was preparing some papers for my father in the Social Security Office in Montevideo. When I saw the steaming boiler pots resting on hot iron plates, it occurred to me that there had to be a better way to heat water.

I dreamed of being an inventor… of creating something important using my creativity. I thought that everything could be improved, bringing progress to the world. I started making prototypes of my idea, and I didn't give up when the first ones failed. Lab tests showed the process contaminated the water, but I kept working until I came up with a design that solved that problem.

After patenting the idea, I started manufacturing and selling my new water heaters, which are still being used forty years later. Even though I benefited from this invention at the time, my priority has never been to exploit it as a business.

I believe my young age and my adventurous spirit had much to do with my lack of concern for personal growth. I had friends working in offices selling heaters on commission. This provided me with enough money for short jaunts to Buenos Aires or Brazil. Sometimes I would ride my motorcycle to Brazil with nothing but a box of heaters that I would sell to hardware stores along the way, making enough to continue my trip into Rio de Janeiro. It was never my intention to grow a business that only now I recognize had the potential to make serious money. At the time, making money was never my main goal, and that has not changed. I lived my life day to day and, most of all, I enjoyed it.

I remember the day I went to register the name "Sun" for my heaters, and I was told that name was already taken. I asked if I could make it an abbreviation, "S.U.N.", and they said yes, but it had to stand for something. So right there on the spot I made up *Soy Una Novedad*, which in Spanish means "I am a novelty".

Back in Uruguay after so many years, I didn't notice any discernable progress. Even my S.U.N. heaters were still being used virtually unchanged. Maybe I've changed. Maybe I wanted to believe I would find things better than when I left. The locals sure didn't seem to notice the lack of progress… the stagnation, and indeed worsening, of the nation. Perhaps having lived in the United States, I've grown accustomed to thinking differently... to thinking of change and progress as a good thing. At that moment, Uruguay felt very small to me.

I talked with friends and family without letting on to how I was feeling, but trying to understand their point of view. I figured they couldn't have noticed the country's slow decline over such a long period of time. I wasn't one to criticize. I left Uruguay when I was young and, although it hurt to see the state my homeland was in, I hadn't earned the right to comment.

How could I criticize a country that, in a way, admired me? Was it not enough that my name would sporadically appear in newspapers and almanacs commending the famous S.U.N., or that I had been named alongside such famous Uruguayans as Artigas or El Negro Rada?

Of course, I brought with me a different way of thinking. I spent more time in the United States than I did in Uruguay, and I was accustomed to a different lifestyle. In the U.S., everything is measured in dollars, while Latin America is based on other principles. Latin American families don't separate in search of opportunities like they do in the U.S., where children are encouraged to go to college and learn to fend for themselves for the first time in their lives. This system forces the child to become independent and learn to blaze his own trail. That's what I did in a country where it was not common. Pushed by the desire for adventure, I left the safety and comfort of home to be myself. Perhaps I was listening to my revolutionary way of thinking... or maybe I was just escaping the discipline and strong character of my mother. These questions were swirling in my mind while recalling these memories of my past. What was I trying to find? Perhaps I was trying to find myself...

I am now living in a country that isn't mine but that I admire and love as if it were. I was able to reach all my goals in terms of career, work and family. I am completely adapted to a society that accepts me and offers the opportunities for which I search. Why is it that I am just now searching for a past that seems so distant and had always been so unimportant to me?

What legacies have I left behind? Family? With the passage of time family has gotten smaller. Memories? I try to find them, but they elude me. Where are my tracks? What horizon was I chasing with such fervor?

At that moment I realized those tracks were all in my mind, and they were etched for no one else but me. The horizon I chased remained in the distance, always just out of reach, increasing my desire to achieve something more. I also realized each human being created his destiny, his future, a way of life. But I could not understand how that poor child, picking through garbage for meager scraps, could ever improve his station in life without being given even a basic foundation that could support his potential ambitions. The poor child was trapped.

I also felt trapped... nauseous... depressed. I was frustrated and felt weak and powerless in a situation that the locals accepted as normal in a country that at one time was rich.

I was born in 1940. An era of prosperity and good fortune for Uruguay began in 1942, when the country was known as "the Switzerland of the Americas." The alignment against Nazi-Fascism during World War II, and the negotiations with the United States and England, led Uruguay to improved standards of living based on the sale of meat and wool to the Allies, as well as support for countries that were in reconstruction or growth phases. This economic prosperity continued from 1947 to 1951 due to Uruguayan exports supporting the countries fighting the Korean War.

Another important factor in Uruguay's economic growth during this period was Great Britain's repayment of debts for Uruguay's support during World War II, by introducing British railroad and water companies. Perhaps these economic pushes made me believe things would continue to advance. I never imagined that in the country where I was born, and where there was always food available for everyone, one would see children eating garbage.

That was the moment when it dawned on me, and with great pain, that the city I had left many years before was in a great decline. Who was responsible? It was a difficult question to answer having been gone for so long. I always kept up with the news from a distance... but now I was there and I couldn't make sense of what I was seeing.

Songwriter Manuel Capella's "*Por la Unión y por la Blanca*" brought me back... El Negro Luz and his clarinet, the Blanditos, La Tota y La Blanca, 8 de Octubre, La Unión, the old bullfight plaza... that was the past I knew and remembered.

While travelling the Americas on my old motorcycle, I had not seen another country like mine until I crossed the border from Mexico into the United States. Was it possible these other countries had also suffered a decline? What would have become of me if I had stayed in Uruguay? Many questions and few answers caused me to fall deeper into my thoughts.

My childhood was not affluent or luxurious in any way. It was simply normal. Even though I was raised in relative poverty, we always had food on our table.

I also recalled my young adulthood, full of adventurous spirit that took me to nearby Buenos Aires or to the farther, more exotic Rio de Janeiro to party at the world famous *Carnaval*.

Rio was my magnet. I had gone so many times and made so many friends in the surrounding cities that I only needed gas money when I wanted to go. Those inexpensive and fun trips were always accompanied by unforgettable anecdotes.

# 2.

# Encounter with the past

Resting in front of a warm fire, my old friend "El Negro Miguel" was startled by a knock on the door. Getting up to answer the door, his bulging eyes betrayed his shock at what he was seeing.

"*Flaco*? Is that you? I can't believe you've returned to our little country! Is that really you?"

Even after so many years, he still called me *Flaco*, meaning "skinny one".

"Of course it's me, my dear *Tierrita*," I responded, using his old nickname, meaning "dirty one".

"But it's been so many years that you left," Miguel said, trying to mentally count them. "Why have you returned?"

"I suppose to visit old friends, my mom, and what little family I have left here," I said.

"I heard you are doing well in the United States," Miguel said. It was more of a question than a statement.

"I can't complain," I responded.

"I also heard you got married and had two boys."

"You're a bit behind the times, Tierrita. Yes, I got married and had two boys, both now professionals. I also became a widower and remarried. What do you think of that?"

While talking about my past with Miguel, the memories raced through my mind at lightning speed. So many years had passed and so many things happened that I found it difficult to use time as a measure to sort all my memories.

Miguel continued asking questions. He wanted to know more about the man standing in front of him after so many years, and each question made me delve deeper into my past. Images of my emigration repeated themselves in my mind, from when I entered the U.S. with only 25 cents in my pocket, to the increasing success of my professional and personal life.

"Do you remember when you took your old Indian motorcycle around the world?" Miguel asked, as if to prompt me into telling tales of that grand adventure.

"Of course I remember. I'll never forget that trip," I responded, secretly happy to have the opportunity to relive such an important part of my life, especially with an old friend.  And so I began…

I've been involved with the sport of motorcycling since I was a young boy. I started with a motorized bicycle that my dad helped me build and, as I grew, so did the cubic centimeters of my bikes. By the time I was 16 I had explored most of Uruguay on my 125 c.c. Motobecane, along with Miguel and two other friends. Those early travelling experiences bred within me the desire to expand my boundaries beyond Argentina and Brazil.

Two years later, I was No. 76 in the Uruguayan Motorcyclist's Center 500 c.c. category. Maintenance of my Norton 500 was a financial struggle, and I took on any odd jobs I could to keep it up. I sold clothing door-to-door for Yaco, a friend of the family's; I worked and learned much about the art of sculpture in Don Vero's workshop; and I continued to work on the S.U.N. water heater.

The conversation continued, and Miguel's curiosity grew by the minute. He would repeat his questions, perhaps only to hear the tales again and again or perhaps because he was a part of my past… and of some of the stories.

My early travels had been with Miguel, and we had much in common. Whenever I would think of him, my mind would inevitably wander to the memories of my cross-continental adventure and to how that led to my emigration.

"Have you seen Manuel?" Miguel asked.

"Yes, I saw him recently in Rio. He's a policeman and has five kids!" I said with a laugh.

Manuel Capelo was a friend of mine who lived in the modest town of Cascadura near Rio de Janeiro. I got to know him during my many trips to Brazil. He was my age, and was a former youth boxing champion as well as a music composer for a popular Brazilian carnival samba school. He served as my guide every time I travelled there, which was almost always on my motorcycle.

I continued my tale…

# 3.

# Planning a crazy adventure

It was hot in Cascadura on the day I was painting letters on the fenders of my old 1947 Indian Chief.

"What are you doing?" Manuel asked.

"I'm going to travel around the world on my motorcycle," I responded casually.

On that particular trip to Brazil I had suffered from hunger. My adventurous spirit had then made me realize that I could be hungry while still travelling to other exotic locations, seeing other cultures, and meeting other people.

I never second-guessed my decisions back then, so once I had made up my mind, I put my decisions to work. That was my nature, and I couldn't change even if those decisions would lead to trouble.

Manuel couldn't believe what he was hearing. He asked the same question again, and again received the same answer.

"I'm suffering on this trip. What's the difference if I suffer here, or somewhere else?"

Most would call me crazy, or thought it was stupid to try to make a trip like that without money. However, I had made my decision, and no one would change my mind.

"You either do things, or you don't!" I said enthusiastically, successfully convincing myself. Apparently those words also convinced my Brazilian friend, for he immediately asked if he could join me.

As I finished painting the words "Around the World" in various languages on my bike's fender, I explained to Manuel how hard this little adventure would be with practically no money. I thought about how Manuel may not be able to handle the rigors of this trip as well as I could. I was 24 years old and was experienced in difficult journeys, having already travelled with little money, and already had a good idea of what awaited me in countries whose residents didn't even speak my language.

After Manuel decided to go with me and promised not to give up, I said, "Well, we leave for Montevideo the day after tomorrow. Bring all the paperwork necessary to get you a passport at the Brazilian consulate in Uruguay."

"I'd like to visit my friend Wilson before we go," Manuel stated.

"Who's Wilson?" I asked.

"Wilson is a man who can foretell the future," he began enthusiastically. "He's the one who predicted Kennedy's assassination a week before it happened! He even once told me that my father was in an accident, and sure enough when I got home that day, I was told that he had indeed been in an accident!"

"And you believe in his power?" I asked skeptically.

"Of course I do! Do you think I can deny his power after what I have experienced with him?" he asked.

"Ok then. We'll go see your friend," I said.

We soon arrived at the foot of one of the many shanty towns of Rio de Janeiro. Wilson's house was not much more than a dilapidated shack. Wilson came out to greet us when he heard the rumbling of the motorcycle.

"Hello! How are you?" Wilson saluted in Portuguese.

"Very well!" Manuel responded cheerfully.

We entered the house and Manuel immediately began telling his friend of our grand plans. Wilson took a glass of water, and while looking through it began predicting the future of our journey.

I didn't pay much attention to his predictions, being a skeptic of such things. Wilson said we'd have to be prepared to endure many hardships, including intensely hot and cold temperatures, hunger, heavy rains, snow storms, and other inclement weather. He also added that we'd be involved in a war, but without major consequences for us.

He opened a drawer and pulled out a pendant hanging on a leather cord and handed it to Manuel. "With this around your neck, you will be protected on your journey," he said. "Never take it off."

I understood everything that Wilson said in Portuguese, even with his oversized jowls that gave him the appearance of an alien. I knew our trip would be difficult, and I wasn't totally convinced we could pull it off. But my pride and ego pushed those thoughts aside. It was clear to me that this part of my life would not be easy, but my enthusiasm for new adventures outweighed any apprehensions I may have been having. As we left Wilson's, I almost laughed at Manuel's strong belief in him.

The next day Manuel showed up with some clothes, his documents, and a small amount of money. We hopped on my motorcycle and took off, leaving in our wake the low rumble from the bike's exhaust, and tears in the eyes of Manuel's parents.

The trail through Brazil was easy going due to the many friends I had made during other trips. We always had some food to eat and a place to sleep.

Our first sign of trouble occurred when we reached the Uruguayan border near Rivera. The customs official wouldn't let us pass, alleging we had to return via the same route we entered Brazil, near Chuy, which was several miles away.

I complained, until the customs official became angered and threatened me at gunpoint. We had no choice but to accept his decision.

We headed for the Chuy crossing, and after a few miles we spotted a small boat on the banks of the river.

"Look at that boat," I said to my Brazilian friend. "Do you have the courage to cross the river in the boat?"

Manuel looked baffled... it was the same look he gave me when I told him I was going to go around the world on my motorcycle.

I repeated, "Do you have the balls to lift my Indian onto the boat and cross the river into Uruguay so we can get off this fucking road?"

Still in shock, Manuel managed a barely audible "Yes. But how will we do it?"

"We'll borrow this boat, put my bike in it, and row to the other side. We'll leave the boat on the other side of the river for the owner... and we'll already be in Uruguay. Way faster than continuing on this road."

We moved near the boat and tried to lift the Indian to no avail. It was just too heavy.

"If we can find a piece of wood we could make a ramp," I said, looking around hopefully.

I couldn't believe it when a few minutes later Manuel showed up with a piece of wood large enough, although it did seem a bit weak to hold the bike's weight.

"Look at this!" he said enthusiastically. "Will this work?"

"Sure it'll work... if it doesn't shatter under the weight!"

We untied a rope from the front of the boat and tied it to the back. We then attached the other end to a stake in the ground to secure the boat. The board Manuel found was then leaned up on the edge of the boat, forming a ramp.

"Ok... push!" I told Manuel while I guided the Indian from the front.

"Let's go! 1... 2... 3... now!" he cried, giving it his all.

The wheels started to slowly turn, and with much effort, we finally got the bike into the boat. We untied the boat and pushed it into the river. We rowed slowly, and with much difficulty, until we finally reached the Uruguayan side.

"Can you imagine what the owner is going to think when he comes looking for his boat and finds it on the other side of the river? He's going to think it was moved by magic!" we laughed.

The wide tires of the Indian now rolled on green grass alongside a wire fence. The fields were so large we were thinking we would have to ride for days before reaching civilization.

When nighttime arrived, we found ourselves in a pasture where cattle grazed. I suggested we camp here, and check out the fence boundaries in the morning.

"What if the cows walk on us?" Manuel asked with a fearful stare.

"The cows are smarter than you think, don't worry. Get some rest. Who knows what adventures await us tomorrow!"

We ate some *rapadura*, a burnt sugar snack we bought only because it was cheap, and prepared to spend the night under a starry sky, each of us secretly hoping the cows really were smarter than we believed.

With perfect timing, a shooting star streaked across the night sky. Finding a decent road to travel on the next day was my only wish. It would be all I needed to make me happy.

We awoke to the light of dawn, and after a bit more *rapadura* for breakfast, we continued our search for a road to Montevideo. Wherever there was cattle, we figured, there had to be people... and where there are people, there are roads.

We passed by many wire gates, called *tranqueras*, which separated different plots of land and gave access to the neighboring fields. Finally, a cloud of dust in the distance betrayed the presence of a vehicle on a dusty road.

"See! I told you! With patience comes reward. That's how life is... things don't just come to you... you have to seek them out. Remember that," I counseled.

"That's why we're taking this journey," Manuel responded.

"Logically. We either do this or we don't. Who knows, one day we may have tons of money and be able to travel in style, but we won't have the comfort of youth. Besides, we would never have gotten to visit this pleasant little dusty road."

We continued on that road until we arrived at a small and rather primitive looking countryside store. We were relieved to find we could refuel the near empty Indian.

The store owner, Don Pepe, guided us.

"Follow this road and you'll reach Minas de Corrales. There you'll find a sign that will point you to Tacuarembó."

"How far is it to Minas de Corrales?" I asked.

"Only a few *leguas*, not too far," he replied.

The same thing happened when I asked the distance to Tacuarembó, so I stopped asking. I knew that country people used *leguas* to measure distance, but I didn't feel like getting into just what a *legua* was equal to.

For Manuel, Tacuarembó didn't mean anything, but I certainly recognized the name. It was a place I visited a long time ago with my friends Miguel, Cacho Fontana, and Carlos Chijani.

Don Pepe's directions were spot on and we reached Tacuarembó in little time. From there, the road to the capital was paved and much more comfortable than the pothole-ridden dirt paths we had been travelling on.

We sang and we laughed so hard we could hardly stop when we thought of how we bettered the customs official that wouldn't let us pass at Santa Ana do Livramento.

I was on my home turf and relieved I would soon be home, even though I wouldn't be there for long. What would my parents and friends say of the adventure we were about to embark on?

Every single one of the Brazilian friends we had visited on the ride back to Uruguay told us our plan was crazy, and impossible to do with so little money. I didn't worry about their opinions, or about the lack of funds. I had already prepared myself mentally to believe that seemingly impossible odds would never be a barrier to achieving my dreams.

The powerful engine on my Indian roared loudly outside my house until my parents came out to greet us. After the hugs and introductions, my parents asked why I had "Around the world" painted on my bike's fenders in Spanish, English, French, and Portuguese. The explanation was quick and without preambles, though my parents couldn't quite comprehend what they were hearing.

We got similar reactions when we told other friends and relatives. For them, it was simply a careless, dangerous, and seemingly impossible journey to take without money. There was a generally pessimistic reaction from everyone who found out about our plans. They all said the same thing. "A rich man's journey with a poor man's odds."

Manuel and I started to study maps to figure out a route that would have neither a starting time nor a return time. I had always said that the only time was now, today and every day. That's how I wanted to live my life.

"Let's go, Brazilian," I called to Manuel, waking him up. "We have to be at the hospital for our vaccines by 8:30."

"You sure we won't get sick with so many vaccines at once?" he asked.

"Come on, don't be a sissy. They're necessary. It will help us survive."

"Ok, let's go," he gave in, and we were off for the hospital.

We got a total of nine vaccinations, and only one of them made us feel nauseous.

The lush tree in front of my house at 3035 Francisco Rodrigo served as our office, and under its friendly shade we planned our future and uncertain adventures. We took advantage of the moonlit nights and sat at the beach in Montevideo. Although we were almost always accompanied by beautiful girls, our minds were nonetheless preoccupied with thoughts of our upcoming journey.

Passports and visas were other formalities that took time. Our start time kept getting delayed, to the point where Manuel was getting desperate... and honestly, so was I.

We mounted a wooden box to the rear fender of the Indian, and on each side we installed U.S. military grade Jeep gas tanks. Hopefully we'd be able to fill them with extra gasoline if we had the good fortune to come across a Good Samaritan willing to help us along the way. The box had room for two small suitcases, and it had two small partitions where we could keep spare bike parts and hopefully any donated canned food.

The fact that we were counting on help from others did not escape us. Neither did the anxiety we felt not knowing how we'd even be received in these foreign lands we were about to explore.

We had everything planned and ready for the departure when I received a phone call from a man who wanted to buy the S.U.N. patent. I calmly told him that I'd be interested if he agreed to two things... the price I requested, and that the entire transaction could be completed within the next three days since I was leaving the country and had no idea when I'd be back.

The next day I received a call that my terms had been accepted. My uncle Ruben, a lawyer, handled the paperwork. Monthly payments would be made to my father, and this eased my mind a bit, knowing that at least some money would be a phone call away in case of emergency. We had already made our plans, however, and with only $40 between us we prepared to leave Montevideo and begin the greatest adventure of our lives.

# 4.

# The Great Adventure

The time had finally come. On the 12th of September, 1964, the day of our departure, friends, neighbors, and family gathered around us to witness the event. Among them was my friend Horacio "El Chiquito" Costas, the famous Uruguayan motorcycle racing champion. He asked if he could ride the Indian around the block to test her out.

"You won't even reach Colonia with this," he remarked after returning.

"You think?" I asked in a mocking tone.

"The front tire hardly touches the road, the rear is too heavy," Horacio declared.

"Well I guess we won't be spending money on tires, then!" I joked.

Horacio's comment had actually bothered me a bit, but I was already used to the negativism surrounding our plans, so I brushed it off. Rather than bring me down or kill my spirit, comments like these usually had the opposite effect on me. It made me want to prove myself… to show it could be done, no matter the odds.

After kissing my parents, and hugging my good friends goodbye, we mounted the Indian, and with her great 1200 c.c. roar, we embarked on our first leg… to Colonia del Sacramento, the gateway to Buenos Aires.

We took a ferry boat from Colonia to Buenos Aires, and when I arrived, I felt very small. In the past, whenever I had come through Buenos Aires, it was on my way back home. This time, however, it was a great bridge to the unknown.

I looked around ecstatically as people were seemingly devoured by the subway entrance and well dressed businessmen walked down Florida Street, as if I had never witnessed these scenes before. Of course, the circumstances this time around were very different and I realized then that the adventure we were embarking upon would take getting used to.

I began writing in my journal:

*September 12, 1964*

*Buenos Aires - Today you seem much larger. Perhaps it's the fear and anxiety of leaving what I am familiar with. I see you as the dividing line between my world and the great unknown.*

*Your lights and streets restrain me. "9 de Julio" seems wider, and your people more indifferent. Your impressive city makes me feel vulnerable.*

*I am wandering your streets now with the desire to see you again, and to keep you in my thoughts for the rest of my trip, and perhaps the rest of my life.*

I finished the entry with the phrase:

*Without a doubt, you are the capital of Latin America.*

The few days we were there were mostly for Manuel to get to know this great city, and for me to reminisce about my many travels there. Like all great cities, Buenos Aires always beckoned for a return visit, although this time, my return was uncertain.

When we left for Mendoza to cross the Andes, we stopped at a small bar to celebrate Manuel's birthday. This seemingly mundane decision had unknowingly changed the course of our travels.

"Where are you headed?" asked one of the patrons in the bar.

"Right now, Mendoza," I responded. "Then to Chile and north from there."

"You're leaving Argentina without visiting Córdoba?" the man asked, curious about our travel plans.

"What's in Córdoba?" I asked, returning his curiosity.

"To not know Córdoba is to not know Argentina," he said, and elaborated with glorifying tourist talk and travel agency details.

In that same bar we met two professional soccer players celebrating their new Bolivian contract. They told us they were headed to La Paz the next day, where they would play for one season. They gave us their soon-to-be address in case we were ever in Bolivia.

A course change didn't really bother us. Although we didn't plan on going to Bolivia, we decided to take the northern route and witness the wonderful Córdoban splendors so beautifully described to us by our new bar friend. We would then return to cross the Andes as originally planned.

*September 17, 1964*

*Today we celebrated Manuel's birthday in a sad little roadside bar. Appeasing our nostalgic sentiments, we bought a small sweet cake and stuck a match in it like a little candle. He blew it out to the sound of my applause and the curious stares of the locals.*

*I noticed Manuel's eyes glistening, holding back tears. These are the difficult moments where we remember what we are leaving behind.*

The beautiful majestic valleys extended beyond the horizon, and the road we rode on was as flat as a billiard table. Suddenly, and without notice, the road became a dangerous desert of loose sand, and the Indian quickly began to skid. It happened so fast I didn't have time to even realize what was happening.

It was the struggle of man against catastrophe, against an accident that could have been avoided with a simple well placed warning sign, against someone's lack of responsibility.

I lost that struggle… and lost control of the bike. It was the first fall of the trip.

"This is incredible," I said lying on the sandy road, unable to move as my right ankle was pinned by the motorcycle.

"Son of a bitch!" Manuel screamed from a distance, having been thrown from the bike, but was luckily uninjured.

"Lift the motorcycle!" I begged Manuel. He struggled but couldn't quite lift the heavy machine off of me.

"Empty the box and remove the extra gas tanks!" I pleaded desperately.

"Alright alright," he said hurriedly as he worked to lighten the behemoth and free me.

*September 18, 1964*

*Today was a bad day. We suffered a fall that left me with a swollen right ankle. When the road changed from pavement to fine sand, a struggle began against the road, against the unanticipated, against our very destiny.*

*The wheels of the Indian started to skid until I could no longer delay the fall. Fuck, what a fall! I can't understand why there was no warning sign.*

*We continued on the sandy road slowly until we arrived at Termas de Rio Hondo that night.*

*We found a small lean-to near one of the town entrances where we could spend the night without having to build our tent. I soaked my ankle in the small thermal pools, which provided some relief. The water was very hot, but the pain of my ankle was greater than the burning. I hope it heals fast so we can continue our trip. For now, we're going to rest.*

Our sleep preparations turned into an interesting conversation.

"Umm, listen... this dog is talking... " Manuel said while staring at the dog sleeping near us.

"Fuck you, Brazilian. Let me sleep."

"No really. I tell you, this dog is talking!"

"Seriously, let me sleep. I'm tired and my ankle is killing me."

"That son of a bitch dog is talking!" he repeated, now in Spanish.

"I told you to fuck off and let me sleep. Dogs don't talk!"

"Fine. Don't believe me. But the fucking dog talks," he insisted.

We didn't realize until the next morning when we saw a man come out from behind the lean-to that the dog's voice and the man's was one and the same. The man was apparently a sleep-talker.

During our short stay, we learned a lot about the inhabitants of that small town, located in the province of Santiago del Estero in the subtropical zone of the endless Argentine Republic. The only cold water they were familiar with was refrigerated... the water in that town was naturally warm. Their teeth were a bright white rather than a normal ivory color, probably due to the strange properties of the local water.

Incredibly, my ankle was no longer swollen and the pain had subsided. Well rested, we headed north in search of Córdoba.

Expansive mountainous landscapes began to appear on the clear horizon, and the road began to curve in that special way that made two-wheel travel all the more enjoyable.

The beautiful vistas were worth the detour we took due to our bar friend's enthusiastic descriptions. Any thoughts of turning back flew from our minds as we admired the beautiful scenery and breathtaking landscapes.

The province of Tucumán was reminiscent of a Valentine's heart, with the Sali river piercing it from north to south like a cupid's arrow. Into the river flowed both the mountain rapids, and the tranquil waters of the plains. The clouds kissed the cedar covered mountains, and from this vantage point the spectacular view of the entire Tucumán Valley could be witnessed.

Brown smokestacks from a sugar factory adorned the landscape with its thick columns of smoke. Fields of crops, each a different shade of green, extended into the distance.

"Would you like to appear on television?" a well dressed man asked us on one of the city streets.

"In exchange for what?" I asked without hesitation.

"Well, you tell me," the man replied.

"How about three days in a hotel, food included."

"No problem," the man quickly agreed.

"It's a deal," I told him, hand outstretched, sealing the deal with a firm handshake.

Using the media was something we had hoped and planned for to help us along our trip… a way to eat and rest well before taking on a new day. We also planned to visit canned food companies and gas station central offices to ask for assistance, almost as if this was our daily job.

Everywhere we went that had a TV, we heard announcers promoting the upcoming appearance of the two motorcyclists that were travelling around the world. We felt very important and almost famous.

The night we were to be presented finally came, and they blocked off a section of road in front of the TV station, where they had set up cameras and lights to capture live the appearance of the old Indian Chief that was travelling the world.

"What do you think, Brazilian? We're famous!" I said smiling.

"Very famous," he replied, wide-eyed.

We arrived in the studio riding our bike and we found ourselves in front of an applauding audience. It was the first time, other than our departure in Uruguay, that we had been in front of cameras. The host enthusiastically interviewed us about our adventure, specifically asking us how we financed the journey. Both the host and the audience were shocked to learn we had undertaken this quest with little to no money.

Between stories, laughs and applause, the segment that made us relatively well known in Tucumán ended.

And so we continued on, searching the limits of the Argentina/Bolivia border. Beyond Tilcara, 82 miles from Jujuy, and about 7000 feet above sea level, where altitude sickness kicks in, we found Humahuaca, a small town surrounded by ancient indigenous cemeteries, steeped in an old and silent history of the battle between the Indians and the White Man. In that most sacred place, I wrote:

*September 27, 1964*

*Humahuaca. We stopped to take in the history... to imagine the ancient lives of the townspeople... their customs, their crafts, their likes, their work. Scholars and historians undoubtedly continue discovering epic and ancient memories buried in places like this.*

*It is specifically for these scholarly types that words are etched in the Pulcará de Tilcara... words written by two renowned wise men: "From the ancient ashes of a dead village emanates the culture of our ancestors, echoes shattering the silence of the ages."*

We continued on to La Quiaca. At the end of Route 9, at 11,293 feet above sea level, a bridge signaled the borderline between Argentina and Bolivia. We crossed over into Villazón, a poor and picturesque village, seeming almost out of place on this deserted path to the north.

*September 28, 1964*

*Villazón. We experienced our first mechanical failure with the rupture of the generator. We needed a repair shop, but the townspeople warned us that the owner of the only garage in town had died and it was now being run by his 10 year old daughter.*

*Being our only option, we had no choice. We took the Indian to the shop. To our surprise, the little girl was an expert and had us all fixed up in no time!*

*September 29, 1964*

*We're still in Villazón. We met a friendly Lebanese boy whose family owns a small Lebanese restaurant. I guess we came across as likeable since he invited us to eat there for free.*

*Tomorrow we plan to continue deeper into Bolivia.*

A powerful rainstorm, lightning and all, hit us just as we were nearing the city of Potosí. The sky was completely cloud-covered and I decided to protect myself with a solid black raincoat given to me by a friend who worked at Uruguay's electric company. To help keep warm, I also wrapped a black sweater around my head under my helmet.

Manuel did something similar, wearing two pairs of sweatpants, and also wrapping a sweater around his head. The cold was so intense, we looked for any way to keep warm.

We were a bit confused, and also a little fascinated at how religious the people of this city seemed to be. They all flashed us the sign of the cross as we passed by.

Potosí is set at 15,827 feet above sea level. In its time, it was the most populous city in Bolivia, and one of the most populated cities in the world. It was a beautiful colonial city, unfortunately marred by the obvious lack of maintenance.

We were in the city when our accelerator cable snapped. We started working on a replacement when an old woman came up to us and asked, "Father, can I help you with anything?"

Suddenly I realized why the citizens all flashed us the sign of the cross. With my black clothing, I looked like a Catholic priest!

"No thank you. And please don't call me father. I'm not even married!"

"Oh... I thought... "

"You confused me with a priest. Not even close!" I laughed.

*October 4, 1964*

*This dark afternoon brought us to the Bolivian city of Potosí, which at one time was probably full of attractive and optimistic colonials, but now feels like a city resigned to its own destiny.*

*On the streets of this city we met Rudy. Rudy, like so many others, was curious about our journey around the world.*

*Rudy invited us to spend the night in his house, as he would not be there that night. He even offered us his own bed. We, of course, accepted.*

*After Rudy left the house, we settled in for a peaceful night's sleep. It didn't last, however.*

*At around three in the morning Rudy returned, drunk as a grape. Apparently, the alcohol erased his short term memory and he had no idea who we were or why we were in his house. Angrily, he shouted, "Get out of my house or I'll call the cops!"*

*So again we faced the intense cold of the Andes. Finding a spot outside of town, we set up our tent and stretched out our sleeping bags, all the while wondering how alcohol can affect the human mind in such a strange way. Tonight was one of the coldest nights of our lives.*

*October 5, 1964*

*The night passed and we awoke to welcomed sunlight. Maybe today will be better than yesterday. At least we were happy to be caressed by the sun... even its weak morning light comforted us.*

*These Andean dry dirt roads are surrounded by an impressive loneliness. It's as if all life had disappeared and left no trace of civilization. The silence is deafening, and all we can hear are our own thoughts and memories.*

From that point on we were truly climbing the Andes and found nothing but atrocious roads. We came upon paths of loose sand framed by rocks and dangerous cliffs.

We reached a river, and though the road continued on the other side, we saw no bridge or other means of crossing. It was the first of many.

We used logs as stakes, planting them along a shallow path through the water, marking a route where the Indian could pass without the water short-circuiting the bike's electrical system. We knew that pushing her through the water would otherwise be impossible.

The altitude started to affect us as well as my poor Indian. The bike was easily fixed by opening up the air intake in the carburetor, however our own physical issues were a bit harder to remedy.

A local doctor prescribed us glucose pills with *coramina*, a common altitude sickness medication in the area. Unfortunately, they didn't seem to help at all. We explained our symptoms to a couple of natives and they suggested we chew cocaine leaves mixed with bicarbonate of soda. Worked like a charm! The bubbles mixed with the saliva in our mouths, extracting the active ingredients of the cocaine leaves.

Apparently the indigenous people used cocaine regularly to battle the effects of altitude sickness. So much so that when they invited us to a party that night, there were baskets of cocaine leaves on every table. We also noticed that some of those who chewed the leaves suffered from strange deformations of the mouth.

In each village that we passed we were warned that a revolution against the Bolivian government was imminent. We were unfamiliar with the current political situation in the country, so we continued on to the capital city of La Paz, ignoring the advice from the locals, only to be greeted by war.

Surprised by how deserted the city was, we cruised the streets on the Indian looking for the address given to us by the two Argentine soccer players we met in that bar outside of Buenos Aires.

Suddenly a loud explosion followed by a splash of hot oil assaulted us when a bullet blew a large hole in the Indian's oil tank, just inches from my right knee. A second shot hit the bike's frame and we tumbled to the pavement. The revolution had started.

We realized we were sandwiched between two enemies firing upon each other from hidden barricades in the town's center plaza and the nearby foothills.

The bike on the ground, we tried to literally dodge bullets. Manuel, who had some military training in Brazil, yelled, "Do what I'm doing!" as he dragged himself to the curb for protection.

"Fuck you, Brazilian! We have to run!"

"Do what I say!" he repeated sternly.

Bullets whizzed by from all directions. Without following Manuel's advice, I desperately ran to the sidewalk trying to find an open door or any kind of shelter. I pushed on a door and it opened. I anxiously called to Manuel and he came running. We entered an abandoned house.

From there we could hear the sound of an air strike on those in the mountain barricades. They had no escape. The battle was short, but the human losses were great.

*November 4, 1964*

*Today we lived through a unique experience. In almost all the Bolivian villages we passed we were warned about an impending rebellion to overthrow President Victor Paz Estensoro.*

*Arriving in La Paz, we found a desolate city, paralyzed by fear and smelling of death.*

*A military force had started the much talked about rebellion, but we never thought we'd be so thoroughly involved. We miraculously found shelter and survived.*

*The country is morally destroyed and full of hate and sadness. Crowds gathered at the hospital where they had large blackboards filled with the names of the injured. The cries of the families would get louder when a name got crossed out indicating their death.*

*These sad memories will stay with us forever. Useless war, children without parents, wives without husbands, mothers without sons. All due to interests, political or financial, that can never compensate for the loss of a single human life.*

We were on the street, somewhere between desolation and the pain of many people. When we picked up the Indian we noticed we were missing some belongings, but that was the least of our worries. Our documents were safe in the metal Army bullet box we had screwed to the handlebars, and our two cameras were with us when we ran for our lives. More importantly, we still had our lives.

The large hole in the oil tank needed to be repaired to be able to continue the trip. Luckily, another biker happened by and stopped to talk to us.

"Are you ok?" he asked.

"We're alive," I answered, "so yeah... we're ok."

"What happened to your bike?" he asked as he eyed the gaping hole in the oil tank.

"A bullet. You know where we can get it fixed? We don't have any money," I stated.

"I have a friend who owns a garage. Follow me."

"How far is it? Can we push the bike there?"

"Sure. It's only three blocks away. I'm sure he can help you."

We arrived exhausted after pushing the heavy Indian way more than the three blocks our new friend had told us. "Herrería Chepe's Garage" was painted on an old piece of rusted tin, and the makeshift sign also listed the services offered. Among them we saw the one we needed... welding.

"Hey José," our new friend Pedro called out. "These two guys are going around the world on that motorcycle, but their oil tank got shot today. They need a favor... and free."

José, also a biker, looked at the huge hole in the tank and said, "We can patch that up. It won't be pretty, but I can weld a piece of metal over the hole so it doesn't leak."

"As long as it's free and doesn't leak, I could care less what it looks like," I said, accepting his generous offer.

After that Good Samaritan fixed us up and we refilled our oil, we lost interest in looking for the address of our two Argentine acquaintances. We thanked Pedro and José and decided to continue west.

Our passage through La Paz was quick, and our only souvenirs were shock, fear, and the sadness of the inhumane.

The roads weren't improving, and neither was the weather. The days were extremely hot and the nights equally cold. The temperatures would seem to abruptly change from a high of over 100 to a low of 32 degrees Fahrenheit. Our dream of a great Pan American highway was quickly turning into a huge nightmare.

At the edge of Lake Titicaca we discovered that the people of this region were resigned to their own destinies. There were no jobs, and the culture looked almost primitive, like an ancient civilization that learned to live on the little they had.

*November 7, 1964*

*Lake Titicaca. This is the highest navigable lake in the world. Its coastline is impressive. Indigenous families live on floating houses made of straw.*

*Every once in a while we see a small native boy tending a herd of llamas or vicuñas. We stopped for gas and chatted with the locals, who spoke Spanish mixed with native languages Quechua or Aymara.*

*It was getting dark and the locals invited us to stay the night in one of their rustic homes bordering a dirt road. As we entered, we noticed the complete lack of furniture, and we were astonished to see that they slept right on the dirt floor... no cots, no hammocks. These were poor and simple people living in a region virtually cut off from the outside world.*

At one end of the lake we found Puno. Although it was the capital of the region, it felt like a desolate village with little life. Most of the inhabitants dressed in colorful garments representative of their folkloric culture. Puno was known as the "Folklore Capital of Peru".

The natives of Puno were a superstitious people. They believed their souls were in danger if their image was captured on film, so they avoided tourist's cameras at all costs.

We followed the rough road until we reached a rudimentary customs checkpoint on the Bolivian/Peruvian border. Riding through, we admired the view of the volcano known as El Misti.

Almost without realizing it, we came upon the city of Arequipa. The second largest city in Peru, Arequipa is built mostly from calcareous stone, earning it its nickname, White City.

We were weary from the events in La Paz and completely exhausted from the over 1500 miles on some of the most inhospitable roads one could imagine.

Since that first fall in Argentina, we had traversed roads covered in sand, dirt, rocks, and mud. We had crossed rivers with no bridges and we struggled with altitude sickness through most of Bolivia. We were ready for a change.

Knowing we'd reach the west coast of South America soon, we stopped in Arequipa for a rest. Strangely, it seemed like most of the people we encountered were showing signs of mental illness.

"Are there a lot of sick people here?" Manuel asked a local. "Aren't there any hospitals?"

"They should quarantine the entire city," the man replied with a toothless grin. "The crazy people here outnumber the sane."

Needless to say, we quickly continued west. We were anxious to reach the other ocean... an ocean unfamiliar to both of us.

# 5.

# The Other Ocean

The Pacific Ocean and a wonderful paved road were waiting for us for our trip to Lima, the capital of Peru. The Indian rolled along so effortlessly that we quickly forgot all about the prior hardships that had led us to this place.

At the edge of that turbulent mass of water, ironically named the Pacific, I sat upon a rock and began to write.

*November 9, 1964*

*We're finally through Hell. We just bathed in the waters of The Other Ocean for the first time. After riding hard on treacherous roads in the Andes Mountains, riding on pavement seems like an unbelievable dream.*

*We're now enjoying the sunny afternoon, but will head out again soon.*

"Kiss the highway," I told my riding partner while kneeling on the asphalt.

"Yes! Finally!" Manuel cried, also kneeling.

"Now we'll be able to cruise for miles without suffering!" I sang while dancing for joy.

"You look like a Bolivian Indian!" Manuel laughed.

"Seems their dancing is contagious!"

We rolled north to the "Thrice Crowned Villa", the nickname given to Lima, the capital of Peru. We found a city of contrasts where colonial architecture mixed with contemporary stylings.

We met up with Eduardo, a photographer for *El Comercio*, one of the most important newspapers in Lima. Eduardo rode a Suzuki motorcycle, and we could tell right off the bat that he was very enthusiastic about our crazy adventure.

*November 10, 1964*

*Lima is a glorious colonial city filled with beautiful gardens and parks. It's been a while since we've enjoyed a real city, and Lima offers us everything.*

*We found lodging at the house of a stranger who was generous enough to put us up. We met Santiago Caballero in a plaza when he, like so many others, became curious about our voyage and began asking us all sorts of questions.*

*The friendly, gentle people of Lima give us hope. That hope encourages us to continue this journey that honestly, up until now has not been the most comfortable.*

*We also met Eduardo Casso, photographer for El Comercio. He interviewed us, and after his article was published, our minor fame allowed us to eat for free in most restaurants in Lima.*

*A store named Batta gave us free shoes and boots, and Don Offrio, a nice old Italian man who owns a cannery and chocolate factory, filled our storage box with canned food.*

Santiago Caballero, the generous soul who put us up in his house in a suburb named La Victoria, made his living as a personal taxi driver, using his beat up old car. We stayed with him during our entire stay in Lima, and we made many friends in that modest little town, including Maria Victoria, one of my many flings during this great adventure.

We stayed in Lima for almost a month, enjoying the picturesque city and learning a bit about the history and traditions of the locals.

With a renewed hunger for the road and for new adventures, we decided to head north. A few days before we left, Eduardo asked if he could join us. I tried to explain to him that if he had the courage to join us, he had to stick it out till the end. Splitting limited resources between two of us was easier than three.

Something told me that Eduardo wouldn't be able to handle the hard road and all the suffering it brought with it. But then I remembered that I felt the same way when Manuel asked to join me, yet together we weathered the worst of storms.

So there we were... two motorcycles and three friends, who from that point on would experience the journey together, discovering new things and making new friends on that uncertain path we were following.

We made short stops in Chimbote, Trujillo, Chiclayo, and Piura, all cities where Eduardo had friends. We soon discovered that our new travelling companion had inherited a chain of over thirty bakeries, and had just as quickly lost them due to bad management. Apparently Eduardo was a dreamer who, upon converting property to cash, would spend it on frivolities and have little left over.

We cruised around the winding cliffs of the Peruvian coast, heading north to Tumbes, a town on the border of Ecuador. The rocky precipice known as Pasamayo loomed before us, dangerously narrow and twisting ahead like a serpent racing along the edge of the ocean.

Our pockets were getting lighter and we were desperate to find a way to make some money. We quickly realized that finding work in Tumbes would be near impossible. These were poor frontier towns where the locals struggled for every meal. No one in that situation would so easily part with something they worked so hard to earn.

*December 12, 1964*

*Luckily, we met a man who owns a circus located a few blocks away... a poor modest circus that could possibly use a new and exotic act!*

*The man showed interest in our story, and agreed to hire us for a few days so we could earn enough to continue our excursion. We can't believe we're now "circus folk".*

*We're being billed as "The Intrepid and Suicidal Bikers" who are travelling the world! But in reality, all we have to do is ride as fast as we can around a track a couple of times. I'm sure our outrageous title is selling them lots of tickets!*

After performing for a few days, we decided we had earned enough to continue north. Once we crossed the Tumbes border into Desaguaderos, we were squarely in Ecuadorian territory, where we were able to cross the Jambeli Channel at Port Bolivar, and make our way to the lovely city of Guayaquil.

As in many other cities, we found lodging in a local fire station. The chief was asking for blood donors for a firefighter who had been in an accident. The humanitarian thing to do was obvious to us so we decided to donate.

Our physical condition was already fairly poor due to the hardships of the road, and when the chief noticed Eduardo's dizziness, he realized that although we gave blood, we had not yet had a bite to eat. It was now the chief's turn to do the humanitarian thing. He gave us 300 *sucres*, the Ecuadorian currency of the time, asking "Are you guys crazy, or do you believe you're made of iron?"

Truth be told, to embark on such a journey you would need lots of iron... the Indian fulfilled that role. But mostly, you had to have an adventurous spirit and a touch of insanity.

Before leaving Guayaquil, we purchased a few shrunken head replicas from a small shop. They were very well crafted from animal leather and bristle, and looked entirely genuine.

### December 16, 1964

*Tonight, during our exploration of this mountainous region, we stopped to sit and watch the stars that mixed with the lights from the neighboring cities.*

*Inner peace washes over us, surrounded by a natural silence that eases our physical and spiritual selves in a way that is hard to put into words.*

*We're each feeling a little homesick, but we're comforted by the true friendships forged by our shared experiences. We are three adventurers united by the dream of exploring other cultures, meeting new and interesting people, and sharing our vivid experiences with anyone who cares to listen.*

*Tomorrow we continue into the unknown.*

The roads became increasingly inhospitable and desolate. The "path of the Indians" was the local nickname of the ancient road that had been created centuries ago by lining up stones in two parallel narrow strips. The Indian's wheels, as well as those of Eduardo's Suzuki, devoured the miles, seeking Quito, the capital of Ecuador. The mountainous path became increasingly difficult, but we continued on into the darkness of night. We could see the lights of the distant city, and reaching it became our primary goal.

As the miles grew shorter, the lights glowed brighter, to the point that we could swear Quito was right in front of us. But the hills and turns mocked us, and we grew weary. We decided to pull over and set up camp.

The next morning we immediately got back on the road only to realize that Quito was actually still quite far away. We learned that it is very difficult to calculate distances accurately at night and in hilly terrain. After a few more hours of riding, the roads were getting noticeably better.

*December 18, 1964*
  *We arrived at the capital of Ecuador at noon today. We decided to stay for a few days in Quito to explore the surrounding areas.*

*December 20, 1964*
  *Today we visited the equator, latitude zero, the imaginary line that divides the Earth. We arrived at the Earth's center point monument just before noon and witnessed the total lack of shadows.*
  *The temperature here is stifling, so we will soon head out for Colombia.*

As soon as we had arrived in Quito, a man approached me and called me by name. I didn't recognize him, but he knew who I was.

"Hello, Carlos," the stranger called.

"Hello," I responded. "Do I know you?"

"No, you don't know me, but I know of your journey," he responded.

"How?"

"I'm a ham radio operator and I communicate with Uruguay regularly. Other hams have told me about you guys."

"It's a pleasure to meet you, then," I said as I shook his hand.

"Pleasure's all mine! My name's Raúl. If you'd like, tonight we can go to my house and you can contact Uruguay."

"Sure!" I replied happily. "Just give us directions and we'll be there!"

Ham radio was the only direct form of communication we had to our families. Sure, we had letters we would send or receive at all the Uruguayan consulates in all the capital cities, but they took forever to go from one point to another.

That night at Raúl's house, we made contact with several Uruguayan hams that successfully rigged microphones and speakers from their radios to my parents' phone line.

On one of the streets in Quito we ran into a local journalist who wanted to write a piece about our travels. Since we already had some experience in this area, we tried to negotiate something in exchange. At the time, we felt very well paid with just a couple of good meals.

We went to the newspaper's offices, where they photographed us while the reporter asked us questions for his story. During the informal interview, I kept exchanging glances with a girl who worked there.

When we left the building I was surprised that the girl followed us out and approached us. Felicia and I began to chat, and in the days we spent in Quito, we became a bit more than friends. She was a single mother who worked in the administration office at the paper and she was dedicated fully to providing for her son. It almost seemed typical of single mothers who had been disappointed in love to neglect themselves in the name of caring for others.

Her story made me reflect on a serious situation that occurred when I was a mere child pretending to be a man. I felt almost relieved when I thought about that fateful decision I had to make when I was too young to find other solutions. I tried to remember what year this happened, and though I can't be sure, I told myself it happened around 1955, when a divorced man with two kids, a son and daughter both about my age, moved in next door.

The daughter, Blanca, had a crush on me, and tried to win me over with sweet looks and coy smiles, but at the time I was with my girlfriend Mary, a brunette from Spain. Blanca once saw me kissing Mary and became jealous, but she didn't stop trying to seduce me.

During one of my break-ups with Mary, Blanca and I became involved. The immature and informal relationship took a serious turn when Blanca told me she was pregnant. Hearing that news at fifteen was like getting punched in the chest. I wasn't ready for this, but I had to face my immaturity once and for all.

The situation constantly in my thoughts, I went for a walk in Rodó Park with my pet monkey Chico. I was astonished when I saw Blanca walking hand in hand with another guy. I went to ask what was going on when the man took a swing at me, which I was lucky to dodge.

Chico, always protective of me, went into a rage and jumped on top of the man and began biting him viciously, chunks of skin flying, while I began giving him the treatment he had planned on giving me.

When two cops arrived, I took off, and soon after I heard the ambulance arrive to take my would-be assailant to the nearest hospital.

Blanca's story ends with the help of an older cousin of mine and an illegal midwife. That phase of my life quickly matured me and left the bitter taste of disappointment in my mouth. I let my memories drift away.

The oil that lubricated the cylinders of the Indian lost viscosity in the heat, and I'm sure she appreciated every minute of rest. The roads remained rocky, desolate, and inhospitable. The nightmare of the Pan American highway was interminable. Our encouragement swelled in the morning after a good night's rest, but deflated at night after a long day of inclement weather and exhaustion, when we would set up camp once again in our rudimentary tent.

We encountered Andean natives with reddish skin, known as *Indios colorados*, or red Indians. The contrast of the primitive and the advanced showed through their nakedness and their wearing of modern watches and jewelry.

On the 27<sup>th</sup> of December, we reached the Colombian border and the roads started to improve. After so many miles of horrible conditions, any minor improvement felt like a miracle to us. We didn't want to remember how the paved Argentine roads had suddenly changed to dirt.

We were close to Cali, a Colombian city 102 miles from Buenaventura, our last South American stop. A few miles before arriving, we spotted several large tents set up by the side of the road... another circus! We figured we could get jobs there while we were in Cali.

We entered one of the tents and saw several monkeys tied to a bench at the waist. Among them was a capuchin which reminded me of my beloved Chico. I went to pet him, but not before I grabbed him by the scruff of the neck to avoid any biting.

A frightened man entered the tent begging us to not pet the monkeys because they were dangerous. Despite his warning, the man was impressed at how I handled the capuchin. We explained that we were looking for work, and he immediately assigned us tasks.

That's how we joined the European Circus of Beasts. My job was to keep the elephants clean and to participate in one of the acts every night. The act consisted of three girl skaters who would ask for a volunteer from the audience. I would be that volunteer. They would grab me by the legs and begin skating in circles, spinning me around and then throwing me into a large container full of sawdust.

"I'm a good clown," I told Manuel and Eduardo, who laughed just as hard as the audience would when I'd get up and shake off the sawdust.

I had befriended a Hungarian animal tamer named Tony, who was trying to tame a young playful bear. One day he asked us to help him get a muzzle on the bear. The plan required five people to try to immobilize the animal. Four of us would hold on to its arms and legs, while Tony would attempt to place the muzzle on him. The little bear cooperated at first, but when Tony attempted to muzzle him, the bear shook violently and we all went flying. No matter how hard Tony tried to tell us that the bear was just being playful, the shock was more convincing than his words.

Another personality that won over my friendship was Enrique, a young chimpanzee from Africa who could not successfully be taught to perform for the circus even though he was very sweet and friendly, and would follow me around wanting to be petted and held. Tony told us that they would often attain chimpanzees from a breeder in St. Louis in the United States where they would breed only the more intelligent simians, but the tamers wouldn't waste time trying to tame animals that didn't seem to have the capacity to learn. Poor Enrique fell into this category.

The circus was large and full of many international performers, living together as one big family, feeling the pain and the joy of every member of the clan. This was certainly true of one of the performers, a Brazilian named Victor Uria.

Victor was a motorcycle acrobat, who would ride inside the "Dome of Death," a huge iron dome large enough for a pair of motorcycles to ride in circles along the inside of the sphere. He would ride around and around while another biker would ride in different directions and come dangerously close to causing a collision. We found out later that Victor's sister had died in one such accident, but he nonetheless kept performing. The riskier the act, the more money the performer would make, so it was very difficult for Victor to justify quitting what had killed his sister, yet makes his living.

Like so many others, Victor would buy gold jewelry and deposit it in a local bank. From there he would transfer money to his homeland. That was how the circus folk ensured their future.

*January 1, 1965*

*Today is the 1ˢᵗ. The sky is draped in a curtain of stars, flickering happily as if to welcome the New Year. Joining in the celebration are the colorful fireworks, the rhythmic clang of distant bells, and the deafening clap of thousands of firecrackers. I nostalgically recall other New Year's celebrations spent with family, friends, and memories of good times.*

One day, while walking along the streets of Cali, I ran into an old motorcycle racing acquaintance I had met in Montevideo. He was a charismatic and friendly man who, upon recognizing me, gave me a big hug as if we were best friends. He invited us for a drink in a fancy bar to reminisce about our old racing days.

*January 9, 1965*

*Today we met with another great disappointment. We ran into an old racing buddy from Montevideo, and he invited us to spend the night in his sister's huge mansion.*

*After a few hours we realized that he was involved in an international prostitution ring, and his "sister" was really his partner in this dirty yet lucrative illegal business.*

*Tomorrow we head for the port of Buenaventura, and then on to Panama. We don't want to be mixed up with these kinds of people.*

The thick Darién Jungle made land travel impossible, so we needed to cross into Panama by boat. We tried to attain free passage in Buenaventura, but were ultimately unsuccessful. We had no choice but to spend all of our circus money on tickets for all of us, including our bikes, to cross.

The boat into Panama was not on a daily schedule, so we had to wait three days before we could leave. We were able to find lodging in the firemen's barracks near the port.

We slept in our sleeping bags on the floor of a large shack. Large rats would come out at night and would crawl all over us, keeping us awake. Eduardo and Miguel decided to sleep sitting up inside a closet to avoid these inconveniences, but since I had trouble sleeping in that position, I had no choice but to risk be awakened time and again by countless rodents.

With little desire, I wrote in my journal.

*January 10, 1965*

*We arrived in Buenaventura, Colombia today, and immediately had to spend most of our money on tickets to cross into Panama, and now we're broke. Tomorrow I'm going to send a telegram to my parents to send us money in Panama.*

With the last of our coins I sent a telegram to my parents to send $200 to Panama. When embarkation day arrived we were informed that the boat needed repairs and would not leave until further notice.

Days passed and our hunger grew. With increasing fatigue and weakness due to lack of food, I wrote:

*January 15, 1965*

*It's been five days since we've eaten anything but "chontaduro", a palm tree fruit, and water. We've been trying to find work washing dishes, cleaning, anything, but with no luck.*

During this frustrating time I thought that human beings were not so human... we weren't begging for handouts... we were asking to trade honest work for a simple plate of food. It was difficult to believe that not a single person would lend us a helping hand.

*January 18, 1965*

*The days pass and the boat is still not repaired. Eduardo managed to find a loaf of bread that we split three ways. We met a photographer who offered to give us food in trade for my camera, but I declined.*

*January 20, 1965*
*It's now been 10 days and our hunger is unbearable. In an act of desperation, I accepted the trade with the photographer and I handed him my "Rolley Flex" camera for a plate of spaghetti, bread, and water for the three of us.*

*These feelings of hatred cannot be measured. We can't believe how a human being, if you could call him that, could take advantage of those less fortunate instead of offering a helping hand.*

It felt like we had been abandoned... like the luck we had experienced earlier on our voyage, had simply run out.

I found a sharp wire that I bent into a hook. I attached it to a long piece of thread, fashioning a rudimentary fishing line. We were, after all, near water, so I figured maybe we could catch our next meal. I successfully rummaged through some trash to look for anything I could use as bait. Unfortunately, after several hours dedicated to fishing, nighttime arrived and we would go to bed hungry once again.

*January 23, 1965*
*It's been 120 days since the start of our adventure. Today I ask myself, "Is this nonsense? Why have we suffered freezing temperatures, hunger, thirst? Why have we battled with muddy, rocky, and sandy roads? Why are we risking our lives?"*

*Today we remain stuck in the ironically named port of Buenaventura on the edge of the Pacific, where the people are not hostile or mean... they are just indifferent.*

*We have to believe that life is what we make it. Is this adventure not life? Or is life itself the greatest adventure of all?*

*January 27, 1965*

*After 17 days of misery, we finally embarked on the steamboat "Bahía Sanguianca" on our way to Panama. The Indian was placed in a large net and lifted by crane, then deposited in the bowels of the boat.*

*During the whole boat ride we were searching furiously for food and the only thing we found was a single bar of cooking chocolate, which we devoured quickly.*

*Sleeping arrangements were small, uncomfortable hammocks. Hungry and bent like a taco, we finally arrived at the port of Panama on a sunny Saturday morning.*

Those 17 days were the hungriest days of our entire journey.

# 6.

# Central America

Arriving in Panama, we felt a renewed optimism, but it didn't last. Banks were closed on Saturdays, which meant another two days of hunger.

Exploring the city streets, I spotted a Uruguayan flag on a door. The sign read "Consulate of the Oriental Republic of Uruguay". Without hesitation, I knocked.

A man dressed in white opened the door and presented himself as Dr. Eduardo Rodrigo Núñez, honorary consul of Uruguay in Panama. I identified myself as a Uruguayan citizen and filled him in on our current situation. I asked to borrow 10 *balboas*, the local currency, and offered one of our remaining cameras as collateral. Dr. Núñez generously handed me 20 *balboas* and would not accept the collateral. I promised to pay him back on Monday once the banks opened.

From there we headed straight to a restaurant.

With full stomachs, we returned to life. We were happy and optimistic… so much so that we even joked about the hunger that had kept us so miserable for so long.

*January 28, 1965*
*We ate today! This is a cause for celebration!*
*Every time we eat we feel like we rule the world. The hunger we suffered in Buenaventura was immense, but now we feel rejuvenated. Our happiness and optimism shows on our faces as we eagerly try to forget the past and move on to the future.*

Enjoying our rejuvenation, we did some sightseeing, visiting Old Panama, the canal, and other points of interest in the city.

Monday came and so did our $200 US dollars. Our first stop was to pay back Dr. Núñez at the Uruguayan

Consulate. After thanking him for his generosity and humanitarianism, we continued as tourists in Panama.

Since Eduardo was a journalist for *El Comercio* in Lima, and I had credentials from Radio CX-8 in Montevideo, we decided to visit The House of Journalists of Panama, an old and famous institution that we had heard a lot about.

The House of Journalists was a meeting place for journalists from around the world, where the protection of the rights and liberties of its members were discussed, and services for all journalists were offered.

We were offered a place to stay in their wonderful Club House. After a few days, we were interviewed by a local radio station about our adventurous expedition, and with that came a bit of recognition and minor fame in that city.

Part of our tourism included the obligatory visit to the impressive Panama Canal, built by the Americans in the early 1900's. We learned that the French had attempted a similar project twice before, but failed due to massive casualties from unknown diseases of the jungle. The Americans, however, came prepared with everything from fumigation techniques to vaccines developed specifically for the project.

We also visited a local Army/Navy store, where we stocked up on inexpensive used supplies, including lightweight aviator jumpsuits, military boots, sleeping bags, and a new tent.

*February 4, 1965*
*It's early morning and we're preparing to move on. We're fully uniformed in bright orange US aviator jumpsuits, which are not only lightweight, but very practical with its multitudes of pockets and Velcro for easy removal.*
*We feel comfortable and important!*

We headed toward the border of Costa Rica. The road was good… straight and paved. We travelled about 40 miles when we reached a police checkpoint. We showed them our papers. Everything checked out and they offered us some soft drinks to quench our thirst.

We continued north and after another 20 miles I noticed something was wrong with the front part of the Indian. Then in a split second, everything turned black.

Much later I found out that when the aftermarket front fork of the Indian snapped that fateful day, we were riding at about 60 miles per hour, taking advantage of the paved roads. At that speed, any minor mechanical fault can turn into tragedy. The weight on the rear of the bike helped keep it from turning end over end.

I instinctually applied what I had learned from my days of motorcycle racing… hold on tight to the handlebars and use the bike's mass as a shield against collisions with other racers. Even though I was unconscious, I never let go of the handlebars.

The Indian had fallen on its right side and Manuel and I slid for 58 yards. When the fork had snapped, the bike lost its front wheel, and my body lurched forward. The camera that was hanging around my neck had smashed against the bullet box mounted between the handlebars, breaking three of my ribs and causing me to lose consciousness.

We were alone with no way to call for help. My body was still, showing serious injuries in the face, right leg, and both arms. Manuel's right hand was rubbed raw where he tried to block his fall. Eduardo, who had witnessed the entire accident, cried and hugged me, fearing for my life. The Indian was on the ground, missing its front wheel and with its front forks totally destroyed.

Fortunately, the same friendly cops we had befriended at the checkpoint earlier that day had arrived in a pickup truck soon after the accident. Without hesitation, they lifted me into the back of the truck, and with Manuel, went searching for medical assistance. Eduardo and his Suzuki stayed with the Indian.

Still unconscious, they drove me north to a local doctor's house that they knew of. A few minutes later, the pickup truck returned to where Eduardo was and they told him that the doctor was not home, so they were taking us to the main hospital in Panama City. Eduardo decided then and there that he would follow us to the hospital and leave the poor Indian on the lonely road.

All this had occurred due to a serious lack of maintenance. The horrible roads of South America had caused the formation of a small fracture in one of the front forks of the bike, and the subsequent travels had weakened it to the point of breaking.

I had regained consciousness but I could not remember anything that had occurred before or after the accident. I recognized Manuel next to me, and I could recall my parent's names, but I had no idea where I was or what had happened. When Manuel would repeat to me over and over again that we were travelling around the world on a motorcycle, I couldn't understand what he was saying.

As they were carrying me in to the hospital on a stretcher, I saw faces staring, and voices saying "It was a plane crash! Looks like a plane went down!"

I had no idea what was going on. I was scared. What did my body look like if people thought I had been in a plane crash?

I later found out that those comments were made because I had been wearing the orange aviator jumpsuit from the Army/Navy store, and people assumed I was a pilot.

The doctors at the St. Thomas hospital emergency room reviewed my injuries. My right kneecap was fully exposed. The left side of my face had a gash that had severed a ligament, causing my mouth to be off center, completely shifted to one side. My right cheek was bleeding profusely. The only good news was that the X-Rays showed only three broken ribs.

A black female doctor promised to fix my face as best she could, as there was no plastic surgeon available at this hospital. I was more worried about my memory loss than my physical wounds. After a few hours, my memory started to return, and I felt instantly more at ease.

All the local newspapers published photos of the accident on the front page, and everyone wondered how we survived.

The first visitor I had was Dr. Núñez, the generous man who lent us 20 *balboas* to stop our hunger. He seemed fairly well known at the hospital, and I noticed that he was ordering nurses around to ensure that I was well taken care of.

Since my injuries did not affect my ability to write, Manuel brought me my creased and tattered journal.

*February 11, 1965*
*I've been checked into the emergency room at the St. Thomas hospital in Panama City. I have never before been involved in an accident like this. The pain in my chest is constant due to my three broken ribs. My right leg, having had the kneecap exposed, is bandaged and elevated. I also feel pain under the bandages on my face. There*

*are maybe thirty other sick or injured people here, many of which seem worse off than me.*

*Today I found out that pictures of the accident were published in all the newspapers in Panama City. I have to stop writing now. The nurse is here to change my bandages.*

The pain was great, but I can't put into words how happy I was that we had survived. The accident was severe, but in the end things weren't so bad. The stay at the hospital was a privilege. All my hospital roommates shared not only our collective pain, but they also felt like they were taking part in my adventure. When I told them about the hunger we had suffered in Buenaventura, they all began passing down their uneaten trays of food. When I would devour anything they put in front of me, laughter filled the room.

"Hey *Flaco*!" yelled Ramón, who had a broken leg. "Want some more?"

"Of course I do!" I said without hesitation.

"You're going to leave this hospital fat!" he laughed.

"Don't worry and pass me the tray!"

The truth is I was still catching up on all the meals I had missed.

*February 13, 1965*

*I was just visited by Dr. Núñez and the Uruguayan ambassador Félix Pollieri Carrió. They brought me books and we talked about the trip and my home country. Dr. Núñez worried for my health and ordered the nurses to watch over me.*

*Eduardo and Manuel also stopped in for their daily visit and brought along with them a policeman, who I immediately recognized as one of the friendly checkpoint officials. I was happy to see them all, but I was ecstatic when the cop told me that the Indian had been taken to the Panama Police garage, and when I was better, I could use the garage to repair the bike myself.*

The daily suffering continued when the nurses would change my bandages, and it was about to get worse. The nurse on duty told me to lower my leg. It had been 10 days since the accident, and my leg had been elevated the entire time. When I tried to comply with the nurse's instructions, it felt like acid was running through my veins. The pain was so great that for a moment, I thought my leg was broken. Between dizziness and tears the pain began to slowly subside... but not entirely.

*February 20, 1965*
  *Today I was finally able to take my first steps with the help of a walker and the encouragement and applause of my hospital roommates.*
  *They removed the bandages from my face and brought me a mirror. Studying my reflection, I could see that the reconstruction had been great. My left eyebrow was covered in stitches, as was the area under my chin. I still have several bloody scabs, but overall, it's not too bad.*

The food trays continued to pile up on my nightstand. My roommates joked that I was trying to set a Guinness World Record in eating, and they would laugh and applaud every time I emptied another tray.

I continued walking, sometimes without the walker in preparation for the day of my release. Finally, the day came and I couldn't be happier.

*February 27, 1965*
   *Today I was discharged from the hospital and Eduardo came to pick me up on his Suzuki. Rather than return to our room in the House of Journalists, I asked Eduardo to take me directly to the police garage to see the Indian.*

I was hospitalized for a total of 17 days so I was thrilled to finally get to see my old Indian at the garage. The police in Panama used Harley Davidsons and they informed me that it was impossible to order Indian parts, but they would give me a Harley fork in hopes that I could adapt it to the Indian. I had to use my mechanical knowledge to bring her back to life.

The first step was to make two bushings with certain specifications. I made some sketches and went out looking for a machine shop with a lathe. I found one a few blocks away. The owner was napping on a comfy chair under the shade of a lush tree.

"How much would you charge me to make these two bushings?" I asked, handing him my drawings.

"10 *balboas*," he replied sleepily.

"10 *balboas*? This should only take 10 minutes," I said, trying to score a better deal.

"I can give you the material and you can do it yourself for 5... "

"Deal!"

His shop was old. All the machines were powered by a single electric motor and the pulleys moved with flat leather straps. The lathe was so old that the screws were threaded backwards from what was common in a modern machine shop. I was still able to fashion the bushings, but it certainly took longer than 10 minutes.

The new Harley fork was ready and came out better than I had expected. We were ready to continue our journey.

*March 2, 1965*
*Today I was able to call my family from a telephone in the House of Journalists. I let them know that everything was ok and that we would soon continue north. The news of the accident had reached Uruguay, and family and friends were very worried.*

I had heard Eduardo tell Manuel several times that he believed I would end the trip and return to Uruguay after the accident. Manuel told him that he didn't know me very well and the trip would continue. Manuel was right. Still limping and bandaged, I was ready to forge ahead.

Although Eduardo and Manuel were very different, they became close friends and loved each other like brothers. Every time we would arrive in a new city, we'd each make new friends, and would often go our separate ways. But we'd always return to continue the adventure of our journey.

*March 4, 1965*
*The Indian has been repaired and tomorrow we continue on to Costa Rica. Today we said our goodbyes to Dr. Núñez and all our helpful Panamanian friends.*

Without a doubt, these last weeks were difficult, but they were also part of our grand adventure. Truth be told, we also had some great times, and we held on to thoughts of a better tomorrow.

One memory stayed with me through all of this, and it was not the memory of the accident. It was Manuel's prophetic friend Wilson. I was shocked to hear Manuel's confession that on that fateful day, he had forgotten to wear the protective amulet that Wilson had given him. I was skeptical of these types of things, but even as I chalked it up to coincidence, Wilson's predictions did seem to always come true.

How did Wilson predict Kennedy's death? How did he know that Manuel's dad would have an accident? How could he know we'd be involved in a revolution? Why did the accident happen the first time Manuel forgot to wear his protective amulet? These were all very difficult to explain, especially to a skeptic like me.

After our tearful goodbyes in Panama, we started for Costa Rica. We stopped once more at the police checkpoint, had a few drinks with the cops, and then continued on toward the border. When we crossed the bridge over the Teta River, which was the site of the accident, we stopped when we saw the blood stained pavement. We took time to reflect on the fragility of life. Everything could so easily end in the blink of an eye... our adventures, dreams, desires, ambitions... our entire lives.

This time, we crossed the river successfully and continued up a precarious mountain path. The heat was unbearable. The relentless sun unmercifully baked the already dry and dusty road.

Suddenly we heard a noise. I looked down to see that the aluminum casing around the Indian's primary chain had shattered. Apparently the chain had broken and its forceful shock had been too much for the metal housing. One of the few precautions we took before starting this trek was to ensure that we had some spare parts. Luckily we had the foresight to bring a second chain. The problem was that the aluminum housing also served as part of the clutch, and without it, the Indian was dead in its tracks.

We searched for all the broken fragments we could find strewn about the dusty road. The heat was wreaking havoc on our nearly naked bodies. Eduardo went to look for water and came back with a full container. The water was hot, but we didn't care. We drank greedily, and left some water to mix with dirt, forming a sort of muddy adobe that we used to put the pieces of the clutch box back together.

After replacing the chain, we carefully assembled the puzzle that was the clutch box, and tightened it into place with the axle bolts. Thanks to that little improvised repair job, we were able to get to San Jose, Costa Rica.

*March 6, 1965*

*Today we arrived in Costa Rica with the clutch box precariously repaired. We were lucky to find a motorcycle shop nearby.*

*Juan Najarian, the shop's owner, is a Uruguayan who fell in love with a Costa Rican girl, as well as with the country, during a trip to the region. He decided to stay in San Jose, a city where bikes were commonly used, and open up a motorcycle shop to make a decent living.*

*He helped us find a used replacement clutch box, and the Indian is now ready to continue its travels.*

*I find it amazing that so far from my country, we were able to find a compatriot willing and able to help us out.*

What were the chances that we'd find a motorcycle shop run by a Uruguayan just when we needed help? Slim, I thought, so luck must be back on my side.

We were very well treated in San Jose and made many friends. Besides Juan, we met many other friendly locals who showed us all the tourist attractions and frequently invited us to eat with them.

The roads were a dull grey, covered with volcanic ash, which gave San Jose a unique and interesting look.

As always, the day came when we decided to move on. We continued north and the highway extended into the distance, like an umbilical cord connecting all the Central American countries.

The narrow winding jungle paths contrasted with the larger than life backdrop of mountains and volcanoes. These were the special moments when we could enjoy the wind in our faces and nature's visual splendors which seemed painted for our enjoyment alone.

Central America was filled with beautiful landscapes, from endless valleys to green mountains. We crossed her countries and visited her cities, admiring the different customs, fashions, and people.

We would always look for gas company offices in every city in hopes of scoring free gasoline, and would usually find a place to sleep in firehouses or police stations. This kept us in the area and gave us the opportunity to visit nearby local landmarks. Whenever possible, we'd veer off course towards the coast to take a refreshing dip in the ocean.

In Nicaraguan territory we continued to enjoy the winding roads that framed the distant peaks of the majestic Mombacho and Masaya volcanic mountain range. We were in no hurry, exploring the friendly villages and enjoying the countryside. We stayed in Managua, the capital city of

Nicaragua, for a week, where we enjoyed the attention of the friendly people. We then left for Honduras.

Tegucigalpa was surrounded by attractive villages like Valle de Ángeles and Santa Lucía. The old Indian rolled along adventurous roads, and I guided her, gently petting her handlebars, feeling immensely happy. It seemed like I was feeling the motorcycle's emotions, if these old pieces of iron actually had any. I believed they did.

After cruising through Honduras we entered El Salvador, and when we reached the capital, we were offered a place to stay at the police station. They set us up in a room with bunk beds. Eduardo slept on top, Manuel on the bottom.

"Stop moving the bed," Eduardo said to Manuel, more than a little annoyed.

"I'm not moving anything," Manuel replied.

"You just did it again! Stop moving the bed!" Eduardo was getting angry.

"I didn't move a thing!" Manuel repeated.

The discussion started getting angrier and the volume grew to the point that one of the officers entered the room asking what the problem was.

"This one," Eduardo began, "keeps moving the bed and not letting me sleep!"

"He's not moving anything," the policeman explained. "Those are tremors, common in this area." That ended the debate.

In every country we entered we had to go to its capital and attain a visa to be able to enter the next country. This was a common occurrence, especially in Central America, where you'd cross a border every few hours. We would get visas for upcoming countries as we needed them, but we planned ahead and got our United States visas in Uruguay before we even left.

When we arrived at the Guatemalan border, the border patrol agent that checked our papers gave us bad news. According to him, our visas were not properly made and he said we would have to return to Tegucigalpa to get new ones. We started to argue but had no luck.

Manuel, using his Brazilian accent, spoke to the official.

"Look, sir, we have to get to Mexico in time to deliver authentic shrunken heads from the Jibaro Indians of Brazil to one of the museums in Mexico City. They are expecting us."

"Yeah, right." He didn't sound convinced.

"It's true, sir. These heads are very valuable and they are counting on us."

"Ok then… show me the heads," the officer said, smiling.

Manuel rushed to the motorcycle and grabbed one of the souvenir heads we bought in Guayaquil, Ecuador. He very carefully carried it over to the officer and gingerly placed it in his hands, saying to be extremely careful because it was very fragile and extremely valuable.

"My god… it's true!" he said enthusiastically, holding what he thought to be an extremely rare artifact in his hands.

"I told you," Manuel said, playing it up, acting proud.

"How many do you have?"

"We have three, but we promised two to the museum."

Eduardo and I could not believe what was happening. Obviously, we knew what Manuel was saying was an outright lie, but it was so intricate and perfectly carried out. We were stunned.

"I'll make you a deal," Manuel offered.

"What?" the man asked, still ogling the shrunken head in his hands.

"If you let us enter the country and give us 200 *quetzales*, you can keep that head." Manuel didn't even flinch.

"Deal!" he yelled quickly, as if trying to seal the deal before Manuel changed his mind.

The officer reached into his pocket and took out a large roll of bills. He gave 200 to Manuel, stamped our passports, and let us through.

*March 19, 1965*
*Manuel just saved us many miles of travelling by trading a fake shrunken head that we bought cheap, for entrance to Guatemala, plus he even made some money in the process.*

*This showed us that greed and ambition is stronger than what should be the fundamental basis for a better world... decency and honor.*

We stayed in a huge hall in the fire station in Guatemala. The hall doubled as a practice room for a group of marimba players. A marimba is like a xylophone, but made entirely of wood and with a large resonating box underneath. The quality of the wood and the design of the instrument made for a unique and enchanting sound. Of course, like with any musical instrument, it also depended on who was playing it.

We slept surrounded by seven large marimbas. The next day, the musicians arrived for practice and we were formally introduced.

Their practice began with a friendly dedication to the three "risk-taking bikers travelling around the world". Manuel, being a composer, and I, an amateur musician, listened intently at the sweet and well played melodies emanating from these uncommon instruments.

We stayed a few more days in Guatemala enjoying many local points of interest.

# 7.

# Mexico

We crossed the border in Tapachula and entered Mexican territory. We followed the road into Tuxtla Gutiérrez and began searching for the northwest route to Veracruz. The caring nature of the Mexican people filled us with joy from the very moment we rolled into their country.

A young man noticed the license plate on the back of the Indian and introduced himself. He was a famous Uruguayan soccer player who went to play for Mexico and now lived in Veracruz. He kindly invited us to stay in his house, which he shared with a Mexican named Julio, a waiter at a fancy beach restaurant. We'd go there every night to admire the ocean view and Julio would sneak us plates of delicious, and obviously expensive, hors d'oeuvres.

*March 24, 1965*
*Today we met Majesky, a Uruguayan soccer star interested in our adventure. He invited us for drinks, and we talked at length about every detail of our journey up until reaching Veracruz.*
*I'm enjoying the company of another fellow Uruguayan living far away from, and missing, his homeland.*

After spending a few days in that picturesque city, we continued on to the capital, locally known as the D.F. for "Distrito Federal", or Federal District.

As we entered the city that hot afternoon, a motorcycle cop, sporting a powerful and new Harley Davidson, pulled us over, lights flashing, sirens blaring.

"Is there a problem, officer?" I asked nervously.

"Not at all. I stopped you out of curiosity. Where are you coming from?" he asked.

"Well, we departed from Brazil, and as you can see, we've travelled through many other countries on the way."

"Where are you from?"

"Manuel is Brazilian, Eduardo is Peruvian, and I'm Uruguayan," I responded.

"Let's go get a drink," the policeman offered.

"Sure," I accepted, not even bothering to ask my riding companions.

We parked all three bikes on the side of the road, and crossed the street to a nearby bar. After a few drinks, and a few more stories of our trip, the cop asked us to follow him to the Federal District Motorized Police Station. We were introduced to his commanding officer, who graciously offered us a room in their barracks.

This place was amazing. It contained four hundred motorcycles belonging to a number of different squads. Each squad was headed by a commander with twenty officers under him. We were surrounded by bikers who could identify with us, and felt a deep camaraderie with these fellow motorcycle enthusiasts. I was starting to believe that Mexican people are just naturally friendly.

My poor Indian must have felt ashamed being surrounded by so many new, shiny two-wheeled machines of power. Or was it me?

We spent our first night in our quarters, and early in the morning we were awakened by one of the commanders, inviting us to breakfast with his squadron. The Indian soon found herself rolling alongside twenty new Harleys on our way to a mouth-watering breakfast at a nearby restaurant.

Once there, I began telling my repertoire of jokes, much to the delight of the friendly cops. This occurred every day with a different squad, becoming a daily laugh-filled ritual. The Federal District Motorized Police were a close-knit family, infinitely friendly and hospitable, and with a great sense of humor.

There we met an older man who used a cane for feeling his way around as he walked. He was the head mechanic and he was completely blind. I can't remember his name, but I remember his face, and certainly his amazing skill. He was able to completely disassemble, assemble, and repair any Harley by touch alone. His ability solidified another life lesson for us... any obstacles we may face in life can be overcome by hard work and courage. This man was truly an inspiration.

I was looking for a local ham radio operator to help us communicate with my parents like I had done before, and one of the officers gave me a phone number. I called and made arrangements to meet the friendly ham who agreed to lend us his radio.

Later, we arrived at El Pedregal de San Ángel, a rather ritzy neighborhood in Mexico City. When we arrived at the indicated address, a man opened the gates to a luxurious home and introduced himself.

"Welcome! My name is Gaspar Henaine," he said.

"Hi! I'm Carlos, and these are my friends Manuel and Eduardo," I replied. "We're very grateful for your assistance in helping us contact other hams in my country."

"No need to thank me. That's what hams do," he declared.

"Well thank you anyway," I repeated.

We entered the huge house and soon arrived at a room filled with amateur radio equipment. Several trophies and awards were resting on a large bureau.

"As you can probably tell, this is my favorite room," Gaspar proudly stated.

"I can see that! You have a lot of trophies. "

"Yes, due to my profession," he said.

"What do you do?" I asked.

"I'm a movie actor and TV personality. My name is Gaspar Henaine, but I'm more commonly known as Capulina."

"Of course!" I yelled. "I knew you looked familiar!"

We hadn't immediately recognized the famous Capulina. At the time, he was huge in children's programming.

I made contact with hams in Uruguay using the code words "modulated frequency", which cued them to connect their radios to telephones to contact my parents. This practice was illegal according to the Uruguayan communications laws of the time.

Gaspar invited us for drinks, and, like so many others, became fascinated with the details of our voyage. As a "normal" person, he could not fathom how one would make such a long journey with no money. Of course, he had a family and a business to attend to, whereas we had no responsibilities whatsoever.

After a long and sociable conversation, we said our goodbyes and returned to the police station. From there we decided to explore the city and do the tourist thing.

The day came when we decided to continue our trek and leave Mexico City. As we were preparing to leave the police station, I was given an unexpected going away present... a full police uniform, helmet, boots and all. I wore it proudly.

Our next planned stop was Guadalajara in the state of Jalisco. The road was well-paved and the Indian rolled along effortlessly. We rode for about 75 miles when we came upon the site of an accident... an overturned car and a young girl with a broken leg. Her leg clearly showed an exposed fracture and was bleeding liberally. Her companions had been trying to flag down a car in vain to take her to the hospital, which, according to them, was nearby.

Without thinking twice, I jumped off my bike and stood in the middle of the road to try to stop the first car that appeared. Soon, a passenger bus rolled up and I signaled it to stop. It did so, respecting the policeman's uniform I still had on. As an officer of the law, I ordered it to take the wounded girl to the nearest hospital.

It was hard to believe that no one had stopped to help this poor girl for fear of staining their upholstery with blood, whose cleaning cost would be negligible compared to the loss of a human life.

A few miles before reaching Guadalajara, I heard the unmistakable *clack-clack-clacking* sound of a failing crankshaft. Understanding what was occurring inside the Indian's motor, I kept a steady speed to try to minimize the problem and reach the city before total failure.

Upon reaching Guadalajara, we headed straight for that city's motorized police station, as recommended by our friends in the D.F. They greeted us warmly and let us sleep in their workshop. The next day I dismantled the Indian's motor to have a look at the damage. Unfortunately, the crankshaft was beyond repair and needed to be replaced. Finding the specific part in Guadalajara proved impossible, so our only option was to return to Mexico City.

With the help of the police squad I was able to get a free bus ticket back to the D.F. and I left the very next morning. Upon arriving back in the capital city, I went directly to my old police buddies, who again showed their kindness by welcoming me back to our old room.

I searched for a replacement crank in all of Mexico City without any luck. I decided to call our new friend Gaspar to ask if I could use his radio equipment once more to arrange for the replacement crank to be shipped to us from Uruguay. He readily agreed.

Luckily, I was able to make contact with my friend Miguel, who agreed to purchase the part and ship it to Mexico City. It would arrive on an Argentina Airlines flight in a couple of days.

In the meantime, the police commander lent me one of his Harleys to use while I killed time in the city. Interestingly, one of his officers soon found the exact part I needed in a repair shop in the D.F. and offered to take up a collection from all the cops in the squad to be able to buy it for me. I told him thanks, but the part was already on its way from Uruguay.

Later, on one of the city's main streets, I noticed a girl with an armful of packages trying unsuccessfully to open her car door. Being a gentleman, I offered my assistance.

"Let me help you," I said, opening the door for her.

"Oh, thank you so much… as you can see, my hands are full!"

"Not a problem, I'll lend you mine," I quipped.

"Where are you from," she asked.

"I'm from Uruguay… you know, that tiny little country in the southern part of South America."

She smiled. "I never met a Uruguayan before. Can I buy you a drink?"

"Of course. I always enjoy being accompanied by a beautiful woman."

"Great! We can take my car."

"Can you return me to this spot afterwards?" I asked. "My motorcycle is parked here." I motioned towards the Harley.

She quickly glanced at the bike, then back at me.

"Are you a cop?"

"No… but I'm friends with them. They lent me the bike. Long story."

"Well then, now I'm curious to know more about you. Let's go, and I promise to return you to this very spot."

After introducing ourselves, Helena navigated the busy streets of the D.F. until we arrived at a fancy lounge. I felt very underdressed in my jeans and denim shirt. I told her as such, and she said not to worry about it.

Our conversation became very interesting as we told each other about our apparently very different lives. She was a professional school teacher with a good position and a decent life, and I was a simple vagabond biker with dreams of adventure.

We were so deep in conversation we hadn't realized how late it was. Helena asked me what time it was, but I didn't have a watch. She laughed when I confessed that time meant nothing to me since I lived for the moment… that was my philosophy. We agreed to see each other again, and she gave me her phone number then dropped me off.

Time passed and I still had not received the crankshaft from Uruguay. Every day I would go to the airport and wait in vain as each plane arrived, no part in sight. Convinced I was wasting time, and pushed by my cop friends, I decided to finally accept their offer to pool money to buy the part they found in Mexico City.

One of the commanders handed me the collected sum, on behalf of all the squads, and I noticed that it easily exceeded the amount needed to buy the part. The next day, as I had done every day before, I went to the airline to check for the delivery. Incredibly, I was told that they had tracked the missing package and that it was in Australia, and should arrive in two days.

I returned to the headquarters with the news, offering to return their money. The commander gathered all his officers in the courtyard to explain the situation. They all responded that the money would be a gift to make our voyage a little easier, and that they would not accept its return.

At this point, my relationship with Helena had turned romantic. We had gotten together many times, and on one of those occasions she had given me a watch. She said it was so I could learn to live beyond the moment. I did not want to accept the gift, but she insisted.

I started to realize that Helena was a very possessive woman who would make it difficult to continue being with her. Almost every day she would stop by the police station asking for me, and the time we spent together was never enough for her. Although she was a beautiful woman, she was suffocating me. Finally, without saying a word, I decided to just head north to continue conquering my dreams of adventure.

I returned to Guadalajara, and with renewed enthusiasm I repaired the old Indian. That same day, Manuel came up to me.

"Flaco," he called me. "Eduardo was crying and says he wants to go home."

"Well, I expected as much. He's been suffering, and now I think he's homesick," I replied sadly.

"I'm disappointed," Manuel said.

"Manuel, I am also disappointed. Honestly, when we started this trip, I thought YOU wouldn't be able to handle the hardships, but look at all that we have been through together. This isn't for everybody, my friend. We have to let him go if that's his decision. It's his life... his emotions... who are we to try to change that?"

Eduardo approached us as if he knew what we were talking about.

"Flaco, you'll have to forgive me. I can't go on. I miss my life back home, and I think it's time for me to return."

"Eduardo," I said calmly. "It's totally your decision. We warned you in Lima when you joined us that this would not be easy. Best wishes from the both of us, and have a safe voyage home."

I guess it was to be expected that at least one of us would not complete the adventure.

*May 3, 1965*
*Eduardo is returning to Peru regardless of his promise to see this through to the end. Does his desertion mean he's not true to his word? Under no circumstances must we let weakness enter our minds.*

Without bitterness, I gave Eduardo a big hug and wished him a safe trip back. His return should go much easier with all the friends we've made on the way.

Manuel and I spent interesting and even dangerous times in Guadalajara. We made friends with the owner of the ice cream shop we frequented almost every day. One time, Manuel had an altercation with a customer who didn't want Manuel to play a certain song on the jukebox. Apparently, this guy was a bully and everyone was afraid of him. Manuel was a boxing champion in Brazil, and though he was a peaceful man, he didn't take shit from anybody.

He grabbed the bully by the neck and said, in Portuguese, "Hey motherfucker! Who do you think you are?"

The man was speechless and went pale. Here was someone who was not afraid of him, stood up to him, and was leading him to the door, feet off the floor. With a push, we heard a thud as the bully's body hit the sidewalk outside the store.

"Don't show your face around here anymore!" Manuel screamed.

The owner of the ice cream parlor was shaking, his eyes huge, as he warned us that this man had been in prison for murder. We had to be careful.

Another memorable experience in Guadalajara was when we were on a TV show called *Muévanse Todos* (*Everybody Move*). We talked about our trip, and even had the opportunity to sing a song in Portuguese, written by Manuel.

*Ai... como é legal*

*(It's such a good thing)*

*se viajar de motoca... de motoca*

*(to travel by motorcycle)*

*Ai... como é legal*

*(It's such a good thing)*

*se viajar de motoca... de motoca*

*(to travel by motorcycle)*

*O vento vai batendo sobre a nossa cara*

*(The wind in our face)*

*o cabelo sobe mais a gente não paraaaa*

*(Our hair sticking up but the people don't stop)*

*Ai... como é legal*

*(It's such a good thing)*

*se viajar de motoca... de motoca*

*(to travel by motorcycle)*

That interview had made us known in Guadalajara, and a local motorcycle club invited us to one of their meetings. The gathering began in a very formal manner, but ended in a tequila-induced drunken party.

Later, we were cordially invited to a weekend picnic with the club members. We met them the next morning at the foot of a tall mountain, where we enjoyed a succulent breakfast prepared by our new friends. Then they announced that lunch would be served on the mountain's peak. Apparently, they were all mountain climbers. This was truly going to be a different kind of adventure.

We took a big breath and began the climb. Already the silhouettes of the other members of the expedition were shrinking in the distance as they effortlessly conquered this minor obstacle, leaving both me and Manuel to fumble our way up. Though the climb was tiring, it was, overall, fairly easy. We reached the top, where we had lunch and enjoyed mountain climbing stories and anecdotes.

The way down, however, was very difficult and rather frightening since we could not see where to place our feet. The club members had to help us down step by step. Right then and there Manuel and I made an important decision... no more mountains!

Our new friends took up a collection and got us a new rear tire for the Indian since they noticed it was quite worn. The front tire looked fine and didn't need a replacement at this time. No one could fathom how we hadn't experienced a single flat tire so far. This reminded me of my comment to "El Chiquito" Costas on the day of our departure when I said that the front tire would never need to be replaced since it doesn't even touch the ground.

A few days later we continued our northern route, travelling on the western side of the country, bordering the

Pacific Ocean. After enjoying the coastal path for some time, we decided to veer inland to cross the Sonora Desert in search of Tijuana and the United States border.

The heat was unbearable. The desolate highway across the desert would shimmer in the distant horizon, teasing us with a watery optical illusion. The large cacti that adorned the lonely landscape stood majestically along the roadside. At every stop we would jump at imaginary scorpions, knowing that they were indeed one of the biggest dangers in the desert.

We decided to sleep during daylight, and travel at night. It was impossible to find shade in this large wide open expanse. Our tent was our only protection against the beating sun. One would sleep while the other kept watch. We would take turns but it was impossible to rest.

On one of those hot days I inspected the bike's oil and I noticed that it had turned a bronze color. Panicking, I filtered the oil through a sock, thinking the bushings in the engine were wearing down. We later realized that the oil had changed color due to the intense heat of the desert.

One of our necessary jobs whenever we entered a new city was to find a phone book and call the local gasoline company offices. We would arrange a visit to meet with the manager, upon where we would tell our story and ask for a donation of gas and oil. They would usually agree since it made a good story for the local papers and the companies would look very generous and caring.

On one such visit, in the city of Hermosillo, the office manager I spoke with kept smiling. I was too curious and had to ask him what was so funny.

"Oh, I'll let you in on it," he laughed. "Wait a minute… I'll make a phone call and you'll soon see."

He made a quick call and asked for someone to come to his office.

"You'll see," he kept smiling.

"Will you be able to help us with some gas?" I asked.

"Of course. Not a problem. I'll give you a ticket to fill your tank."

"How about... tanks?" I asked, a little embarrassed.

"You have more than one?"

"Yeah, the one on the bike, plus two more containers we carry, like the ones used in the army."

"Not a problem, my friend. Three it is!"

He gave me a piece of paper with his signature and brief directions to where we had to go to fill the tanks. A few minutes later, a man entered the office and I instantly knew what the manager was smiling about. Although this man was a bit older, he could have been my twin! We all had a great laugh, and I joked that my grandfather had also been an adventurer and had passed by Hermosillo several years ago.

We left Hermosillo and continued on towards Tijuana, our final destination inside Mexican territory. We stopped when we saw a VW "Combi" Van with California plates parked on the roadside. A blonde man, or *güero* as the Mexicans called them, was standing next to the vehicle.

"Hello," I said in Spanish, thinking he wouldn't understand me.

"Hello there. Where are you headed?" he asked, in perfect Spanish.

"Well we're travelling around the world and we're now heading north. Are you American?"

"Yes I am, and I'm also travelling north, to California, which is where I live."

"Your Spanish is perfect. Where did you learn to speak so well?" I asked.

"My mother is Mexican, and my father is American. She taught me. Where are you guys from?"

"Manuel is from Brazil, and I am from Uruguay. What's your name?"

"Frank, but you can call me Francisco, which my mother prefers. I have some canned food. Would you like to join me for lunch?"

"It would be our pleasure to have lunch with you. My name is Carlos. Very nice to meet you, Francisco."

Francisco had travelled to Mexico to buy some artwork he planned to bring back to the U.S. for a store he was opening. We had a pleasant meal with him and he invited us to stay at his house whenever we reached Seal Beach. We said our goodbyes, and with a hug we promised to see him again in a few days.

Tijuana seemed like a very poor and disorganized city. They stamped our passports in a little roadside shack on the Mexican side and we crossed the border. That's when we realized that we had overstayed our time in Mexico and that our visas had already expired.

# 8.

# The Impressive United States

We reached the United States border and everything looked different. There was a large concrete office building, uniformed officials, and an order we never witnessed at any other border crossing.

A customs officer began to question us in nearly perfect Spanish. Although we had a visa that allowed us entry, we knew that the final decision was left up to the officer and his opinion of us. The interrogation began.

"Why are you travelling?"

"We're writing about our travel experiences for a book we're working on," I lied.

He asked for proof and I showed him my journal as well as several newspaper clippings from the different countries we had travelled.

"Where do you get your travel money?" he asked.

"We get paid for sending our journal entries for publishing. We work for a television and radio station," I said without hesitation.

He asked for more proof, and I showed him a letter from the Sarandi Radio Station of Montevideo to all amateur radio operators and other radio stations asking for their collaboration in helping us on our trip.

"Do you have other means in case you run short on funds?"

"Sure. I own a factory of water heaters in Uruguay," I said, showing him a copy of the certification of the S.U.N. name.

"How much money do you have on you now?"

We turned white... this was a difficult question to answer. We only had twenty-five cents, which I had in my right pants pocket, and a full tank of gas. Admitting our poverty to the nosey official would surely keep us from crossing the border, I thought. With a cold calmness, and risking that he may request proof like he's been doing, I responded, "Right now we only have $200, but we are expecting a wire at the First National City Bank in Los Angeles."

Surprisingly, he didn't ask for proof and simply stamped our passports. We crossed into the United States.

*June 26, 1965*

*We just crossed the most difficult border in the world. The immigration officer thoroughly interrogated us and wanted to know all about us. We've never seen a border like this!*

*We're now travelling on the San Diego Freeway, and it feels like a dream. We're thrilled to be in this country... this really is different.*

The San Diego Freeway was truly impressive. Wide lanes of asphalt that converged in the horizon... we've never seen anything like this. We started comparing this to the so-called "Pan American Highway" and we had to laugh. There is no comparison.

The road was divided into five lanes going north, five more going south, and multiplied even further with every off-ramp and overpass. Riding on this extraordinary road was easy. At first, when I would see a slight color change in the pavement, I would brace myself for unevenly repaired pot holes. I quickly realized that was unnecessary since the repairs were done with such precision, they must have used a giant spatula to fill in the holes so perfectly. The Indian didn't even flinch as we sped over top of them.

We stopped at a service station to check out what they had, and to clean up and use the restrooms. I went directly to the bathroom while Manuel looked around. When I returned, Manuel's eyes were wide with wonderment.

"Flaco! Look at this! You put a coin in this machine, and a sandwich comes out!"

"That's nothing!" I said. "In the bathroom there's a machine with soft brushes and water that cleans your ass!"

"No way!" he yelled, running for the bathroom to see for himself. Obviously, I was just playing a little joke on my friend who was so impressed by automation.

Arriving in Los Angeles, we realized we were so focused on that as our destination that we had gone about 30 miles north of Seal Beach, where Francisco was expecting us. We hadn't eaten anything and we were almost out of gas.

Sitting on a curb we had to figure out how to get gas money to be able to continue on to meet our friend. In Spanish speaking countries it was relatively easy, but in this place, where we hardly knew a word of English, it was much more difficult.

We put our hopes in two people walking along the other side of the street. They looked like they might be Mexican.

"Do you speak Spanish?" I yelled in Spanish.

When we heard a "yes", it was music to our ears and we quickly crossed the street and struck up a friendly conversation. I explained our difficult situation and asked for one dollar so we could put two gallons of gas in the Indian's nearly empty tank. The two friends took pity on us and gave us a dollar, and also bought us a coffee accompanied by a delicious hamburger. After our meal, we bought our gas and began our short trip back south to Seal Beach.

Seal Beach was a quaint little seaside town south of Los Angeles. We arrived at Francisco's house to be greeted by his son's nanny. She only knew English and communication was difficult. She finally handed us a business card that read *Frank Gary Burden* and contained his phone number.

Finding a telephone booth, we attempted to make contact, but we could not figure out how to place a call successfully. American phone booths worked differently than what we were used to. Luckily, a nice man, seeing us struggling, approached us and invited us to use the phone at his house.

Francisco told us he was at the opening of an art boutique in Newport Beach and we should head over and he'd provide food and drinks. We told him we were not properly dressed nor showered for such an event, as we had just arrived from Mexico. He said not to worry and to stop by anyway.

Surrounded by guests in tuxedoes, we arrived at the boutique in Newport Beach. The place was luxurious and we felt very out of place, but the kindness of all the people put us at ease. At three in the morning we followed Francisco's car back to his house.

Due to the connections we made in Newport Beach, we quickly found work decorating the exterior wall of a house belonging to an actress and her lawyer husband. The couple wanted to decorate the outer wall of their garage, which faced an impressive pool, to look like there was a large wood pile stacked up against it.

It took us over a week to complete, having cut several logs of varying lengths and gluing them all to a wooden baseboard that we then screwed into the wall. With this job, we made our first American dollar.

Later, utilizing the skills that Don Vero had taught me, I started carving wooden figurines to sell at Francisco's art boutique.

*June 30, 1965*

*Today is my 25th birthday. Francisco invited me and Manuel to a dinner party with his wife and a group of friends. We feel right at home surrounded by such friendly people. Although I miss my parents, friends, and country, I'm still very happy I am on this journey. Along the way I have had the pleasure of making friends like Francisco.*

*At the party we met Sharon, an attractive woman who, according to Francisco, was separated from her husband and lived alone. We enjoyed dancing with each other but it was difficult for us to communicate. Because my English is so bad, I use a little pocket dictionary to help me out when I get stuck in a conversation.*

> *I found a pencil and drew on a napkin. I drew a house with the door closed, and with the help from my dictionary, I wrote "Your house" underneath it. Then I drew another house next to it with the door open and wrote "Your house tonight". Obviously, this became the joke of the night and we all had a good laugh.*
>
> *Later at night, I passed by Sharon's house and found her door was open.*

Another night while dining at a couple's house, friends of Francisco's, the lady of the house began rubbing my legs under the table with her feet. I didn't refuse her advances, and the next day she picked me up in her car and took me to a hotel.

These types of situations presented themselves quite often to me and Manuel during our adventure. We were young, and the fact that we were drifters, always on the way to the next town, made us safer targets for the fantasies of bored women.

Walking around Los Angeles we met a reporter who took an interest in our journey. He interviewed us for an extensive story that was published the next day in the Los Angeles News. During the interview we mentioned Francisco, who has been such a great help to us. From the information gathered from the article, a man named Sam Pierce called Francisco and told him he wanted to meet us and help us.

Francisco explained to us that Sam Pierce was a well known figure in the motorcycling world, having won countless races using Indian motorcycles. He now owned one of the biggest motorcycle shops in the Santa Ana area.

Sam was very kind and showed great interest when we discussed our trip with him, especially when we talked about the old Indian. Using a Mexican barber friend of ours as an interpreter, Sam invited us to eat and talk all about our voyage.

"Could you stay in Santa Ana for a few days so I can refurbish your bike?" he asked us.

"Sure, but we don't have much money."

"Don't worry about the money. I'm offering you this free of charge. My wish is that you complete your journey with no mechanical problems."

"Well, then of course we'll stay!" I responded, not believing what he was offering us.

"Ok, let's go ask the Chilean if you can stay at his house while the bike is in the shop."

The Chilean was an employee of Sam's who came to the United States to seek a better future for his family back in Chile. He lived near the Pierce Motor Center, and when asked if he would put us up until the work on the bike was complete, he readily agreed.

I looked in wide-eyed disbelief at the place where the refurbishing was going to take place. It didn't look like a typical garage… it was more like a hospital operation room. The walls and floors were covered in bright white tiles, and white cabinets hung over the workbenches.

We looked stunned when they began taking apart my Indian, taking brand new parts from their original boxes and building a new motor and gearbox. I looked on curiously as they put a white creamy substance on all the parts before assembling them. They later put the bottom part of the engine into a machine that would spin the crank at a predetermined speed for a predetermined amount of time. Then they removed the parts from the machine, disassembled everything, washed all the components, and put it all back together again.

I asked what that was about, and they told me it was how they "softened" the engine. I realized then that the United States had more advanced technology, and an incredible order and cleanliness.

In three days, the Indian had been completely transformed. It had a new motor and transmission, an oil tank without a bullet hole, new sprockets and chain, new tires, a reupholstered seat, and it had even been repainted in its original color. The Indian was never in better shape, and this incredible gift seemed like a dream come true.

*July 8, 1965*
*This is incredible. I was practically given a brand new bike! No one has ever offered us anything close to this. This man, a total stranger to us, offered us everything in exchange for nothing in return. My old Indian is new again. The truth is I was without words to express my gratitude.*

We departed slowly from Sam's garage, leaving the old Indian motor and a picture of us with Sam in the shop window as a symbol of the distance we have travelled. We also left behind Sam himself, who so selflessly helped us… an act we will remember for the rest of our trip, and indeed the rest of our lives.

A few days later, we headed for San Francisco.

VUELTA AL MUNDO

TRIP ROUND THE WORLD

TOUR DU MONDE

VOLTA AO MUNDO

RECUERDO      LEMBRANÇA

SOUVENIR      REMEMBER'S

# LA VUELTA AL MUNDO EN MOTO

Una pareja de jóvenes "trotamundos", conformada por el uruguayo Carlos Alberto Caggiani y el brasileño Manuel Capelo Filho, llegaron a nuestra ciudad en raid motociclístico.

Partieron el 14 de Mayo, desde Río de Janeiro, en donde ambos residen, y hasta el momento llevan recorridos unos 25.000 Kms. (Brasil, Uruguay, Argentina, Bolivia y Perú).

Las aspiraciones de estos dos raidistas es llegar hasta San Francisco (EE. UU.), y de allí embarcarse para Japón, recorriéndose todo el Asia, Europa y Africa.

Calculan que tendrán otro extenso recorrido de 70.000 Kms. y que dentro de un año estarán de regreso al Brasil.

Caggiani, de 24 años, ex estudiante de Agronomía, y Capelo, ex vice-campeón amateur de los Medio Ligeros del Brasil, refirieron una anécdota sobre su paso por Bolivia.

Llegaron en su moto Indian, de 1.200 cc., en días de la revuelta en La Paz. Fueron tiroteados, aunque no sufrieron herida alguna. Pero, una turba, les robó dinero.

Actualmente, se hallan en casa de un ocasional amigo peruano, Santiago Caballero, en un taller de mecánica, sito en Prolongación Huánuco 1354, en El Porvenir.

# En 2 Ruedas Larga Travesía

Un escultor. Otro instructor de boxeo. Ambos con sus optimistas 24 años y un mundo de ilusiones. Comparten el ideal que es su más caro sueño: la vuelta al mundo en motocicleta. Visitas países, otros climas, observar diversas costumbres con el ronroneo de su máquina y al compás vibrante

Tierra del sol naciente, Japón, para enhebrar Asia, luego Europa, Africa, cruzar el Atlántico y volver a tierra Brasileña, en la imaginaria línea en torno al universo.

Dicho así, a grandes rasgos, parece tarea fácil y cómoda. Pero serán nada menos que 75.000 kilómetros. Hubo ya muchas horas de

de sus renovadas ilusiones.

Para "hacer boca" llegaron desde Río de Janeiro, dos meses atrás, a despedirse de familiares y abordar la gran empresa.

San Carlos Alberto Caggiani, el compatriota y Manuel Capelo Filho, el norteño. Desde Montevideo, pasarán a Argentina, luego de la cordillera a Chile y la carretera panamericana rumbo al norte hasta San Francisco de California. En seguida el "salto" del Pacífico hasta la

estudio sobre los mapas, infinidad de gestiones en procura de la mejor información sobre tantos países, religiones, costumbres, política, todo en fin que evite las sorpresas y pueda garantizar —dentro de lo relativo— normalidad en la larga ruta y un final acorde con sus ilusiones.

Así hablaron Caggiani y Capelo. A quienes presentamos con la "poderosa" Harley de las que irán, caballeros, por tantos horizontes.

*Nicaragua*

*Humahuaca, Argentina*

Oil tank bullet hole
*Bolivia*

*Lake Titicaca, Peru*

*Buenaventura, Colombia*

*Panama*

# CASI se MATAN

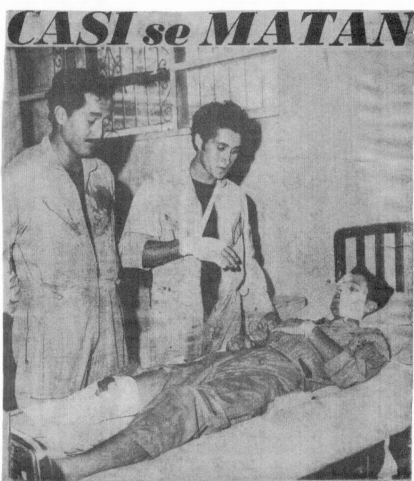

En el Hospital Santo Tomás, fueron atendidos los "raidistas" lesionados.—En la gráfica aparecen desde la izquierda, Leoncio Eduardo Caso, peruano y reportero gráfico de "El Comercio", de Lima; el brasileño Manoel Capelo Filho, hijo de 25 años, y el uruguayo Carlos Alberto Caggiani, de 24 años y quien conducía la moto del accidente. —(Foto Ismael Achurra).

Milagrosamente salvaron la vida ayer, dos raidistas que en un viaje hacia el interior del país sufrieron un aparatoso accidente cuando la motocicleta en que viajaban se salió de la carretera Interamericana en forma aparatosa, causando heridas de cuidado a sus pasajeros.

El accidente ocurrió en el lugar conocido como "Teta" jurisdicción de San Carlos en horas del mediodía y resultaron lesionados el conductor de la moto, Carlos Alberto Caggiani, uruguayo de 24 años con pasaporte de Uruguay número 121675 y su compañero de viaje, el brasile-

ño Manoel Capelo Filho, hijo de 25 años y con pasaporte de su país con el número 436825.

Los heridos y el corresponsal gráfico Leoncio Eduardo Caso, quien salió ileso por viajar en otra moto, fueron conducidos a la ciudad capital por el carro de

(Pasa a la Página 17)

*Tropic of Cancer, Mexico*

*Tijuana, Mexico*

Sam Pierce
*Santa Ana, California*

*Long Beach, California*

# This Man's Home Is His Saddle

By LEONARD HORAK
Staff Writer

Chugging its noisy way through city streets last week was a strange sight.

It wasn't a bird. It wasn't a plane. It wasn't even Superman.

It was 23-year-old Uruguayan Carlos Caggiani on the 1948 motorcycle which is carrying him faithfully—well, almost—around the world.

And behind the well-worn saddle is the tall metal box which he laughingly calls "my home."

The box on the ancient motorcycle has been his "home" since the tall, lanky radio press journalist set out from Montevideo in May, 1964—nearly 200,000 miles ago.

With his faithful steed—the forks broke in Panama and had to be replaced—parked outside the Saint John YMCA on Hazen Avenue, Carlos explained in a mixture of English, Spanish and Italian a few of the incidents that have befallen him on his incredible journey.

Setting off with a Brazilian friend, Manoel Filho, the pair forged northwards along the rock littered roads of the South American interior, crossing the Amazon with a herd of cattle.

Bolivia found them in the middle of a revolution which left them with a bullet hole in the tank as a souvenir, and an accident in Panama resulted in a hospital stay for Carlos.

As time wore on, his friend became saddle-sore and Carlos pushed on through the states to Los Angeles and San Francisco, and on to New York.

Always, there was his "home," the tin box containing a tent, some clothes, and a few spare parts.

Carlos had hoped to sail from San Francisco to Japan and Asia, but he abandoned this plan to turn Eastward instead and finally arrived in Saint John Wednesday.

Now his sights are turned towards Europe, for he and his motorcycle are bound for Dublin, Ireland, on the "Fort Hood."

Carlos, who liked the wealth of the States and the wide roads stayed there for several months, and would like—eventually—to make his home there.

"But Europe", he says with a shrug of the shoulders, "is not so big... maybe three months".

He plans to travel through Ireland, England, France, Holland, Belgium, Germany, Italy, and if he can obtain a visa, Czechoslovakia.

For a man who speaks Spanish, Italian, and Portuguese, Carlos admits that one of the biggest problems on his never-ending trip has been "my bad English".

But his English is improving, and he has proven his ingenuity to carry him through any situation. And there's always the English-Spanish dictionary in case of difficulty.

It must be a happy life, travelling the world, for Carlos seems happy enough, and meanwhile he caused quite a stir in Saint John.

Caggiani And His Cycle

*Paris, France*

# 9.

# San Francisco

The road remained in excellent condition and progress was easy. We veered a bit north and west and entered the magnificent Yosemite National Park. The view was breathtaking. We camped in that beautiful place and enjoyed a well deserved rest.

On one of those nights we were awakened by a noise outside our tent. We peeked through the tent flap and discovered two large black bears licking the dirty pots and pans of our neighbor's camp. We immediately closed the tent and tucked ourselves tightly in our sleeping bags, hoping the bears would leave peacefully.

Arriving in picturesque San Francisco, we headed straight for the Uruguayan consulate to pick up any mail that might be waiting for us, like we've done so many times before when entering a big city. I introduced myself to the secretary and she told us that the consul wasn't in at the moment, but had left instructions to contact him when we arrived. The consul, uncle of my friend Héctor Viglione from Uruguay, had already heard about our adventure. We waited there until the consul arrived.

An adventurous twinkle in his eye, Humberto Viglione entered the room and excitedly greeted us.

"Hello boys! How are you? We have to spend some time together… I must hear all about your adventures!"

"Very pleased to meet you. Your nephew Héctor has told us a lot about you."

"All good, of course?"

"But of course!" we laughed.

Viglione looked me over and declared "You're all skin and bones. What's wrong? Don't you eat?"

"From time to time," I said, trying to add a little humor to my tone.

"Fuck," he said. "I'm serious. Do you want to die?"

"With all respect," I tried to explain. "On this trip one doesn't eat every day. Sometimes it's more important to fuel the one that is ridden than the riders themselves. You know what I mean?"

"You don't have to explain it to me," Viglione replied. "I did the same trip years ago, with no money and on foot."

Humberto Viglione was a character. In his youth he had hitchhiked his way to California. Born in Uruguay, and like us with no money, he travelled all of America, finally settling in San Francisco.

In those days, the city was plagued by rats and the local government would pay for each dead rat in an effort to exterminate the plague. Viglione, with his cowboy mentality and country boy idiosyncrasies, hunted rats for a living.

Being one of the only Uruguayans in the city at the time, he would help any fellow Uruguayan immigrants that would arrive. Still young, he studied diplomacy and eventually became the consul for the Oriental Republic of Uruguay. Simple, lively, and intelligent, he never forgot his past. He was the consul, but above all, he was still a *gaucho*, a Uruguayan cowboy.

Due to his honesty and simplicity, he was known as "El Loco Viglione", or "The Crazy Viglione". This gave him a sort of status that he rather enjoyed. Through hard work and dedication, he achieved the dream of all *gauchos*... he owned three farms outside San Francisco. He cordially invited us to rest at one of his properties.

"You will stay at one of my farms," he insisted. "You're too skinny. You need to rest."

"We only have one problem... lack of funds. So we'd prefer to continue heading to the East Coast," I said.

"Would you like to make some money?" he asked.

"Of course. Who wouldn't?"

"Ok, I'll make you a deal. You will work at one of my farms, and you'll have a place to sleep and food to eat. I have to remain here, but you do the job, and I'll pay you."

"Deal!" Manuel and I said in unison.

"By the way," Viglione continued. "You're in the world of motorcycles... did you know that "El Chiquito" Costas is here?"

"I don't believe it! Seriously?" I asked.

Horacio "El Chiquito" Costas, Uruguayan motorcycle racing champion, was the one who, on the day we started our journey, had test driven the Indian and declared we'd never even reach Colonia. We asked Viglione for Horacio's address, as we planned to surprise our old skeptical friend.

We arrived at an apartment building anxiously awaiting our reunion with "El Chiquito" Costas. We rang the doorbell twice and waited. Horacio opened the door.

"I can't believe it," he said, openly showing his surprise.

"You better believe it!" I said with a touch of sarcasm in my voice.

"You actually did it! How did you make it here on that Indian? I can't believe it!" he repeated.

"Well, we're here now and still have much more travelling ahead of us."

"Come in, come in! I want you to tell me everything about your journey!"

Horacio had to admit that his prediction ten months ago was wrong, and after a big hug, he offered us food and drink in celebration of our arrival in San Francisco. We stayed in his house for a few days, then, as promised, headed to one of Viglione's farms.

Accustomed to seeing farm houses on the outskirts of many towns throughout our trip, we couldn't believe what we were now seeing. Across a stream and centered on a lush green valley we found a beautiful residence which had nothing in common with the common farm houses we were used to.

Later we came to realize that the house's interior was even more luxurious. A color TV, a refrigerator, and even a large freezer full of all kinds of meat, were some of the comforts this house had to offer.

Viglione showed up once a week as promised, with food, payment for our work for that week, and a new job for the next week. One day he told Manuel that he expected us to clean out the two barns where the sheep were kept. After he left, we went to inspect the barns and scope the job. We decided it was impossible to clean both barns in such a short amount of time due to the large amounts of sheep manure that had accumulated over the years. Trying to find a solution to the problem, we explored the surrounding area and found a tractor next to one of the barns.

"Are you thinking what I'm thinking?" I asked Manuel, eyeing the tractor.

"Not sure… what are you thinking?"

"I'm thinking that if that tractor can fit through the barn doors, we can finish this job in less time than it takes a rooster to crow."

"But we don't even know how to drive that thing," Manuel said worriedly.

"It's as good a time as any to learn. Besides, we're in the middle of nowhere so there's no chance we'll kill anyone," I joked.

"You game?"

"Of course I am. The point is to do this job fast and with little effort."

"Should we try now?"

"Let's do it! Measure the tractor's shovel with that rope. Then we'll measure the barn doors."

Manuel grabbed the rope. I held one end on one side of the tractor's big scoop, and he moved to the other side and cut the rope the exact length of the widest part of the tractor. We then quickly took the rope to the nearest barn doors.

"It fits! The tractor's shovel is a little bit smaller than the entrance!" Manuel exclaimed happily.

"Now we have to learn how to drive this beast," I said, moving toward the machine.

I climbed into the tractor. The keys were in the ignition and it started easily. In front of me was a host of levers that I slowly began pulling one by one, carefully, learning which lever moved what. After practicing for a few minutes, we were ready to start the job.

In less than four hours, both barns were completely clean and we had the luxury of resting for the rest of the week. We took some meat from the freezer and improvised a grill with a metal screen we found in one of the barns. We celebrated with a bottle of red wine and a traditional South American barbeque, called a *parrillada*. We even took the Indian out to a nearby town just to have some fun.

Necessity certainly is the mother of invention.

When Viglione returned at the end of the week and saw that both barns were immaculate, he not only congratulated us, but added a little extra to our pay.

That same day Viglione had received a packet of *yerba mate*, a traditional South American tea, from Uruguay. As Viglione could not drink *mate* due to a stomach ailment, he decided to call the new consul of Argentina to offer him the herb since Argentines were also fond of the drink.

He dialed the number and asked to speak to the consul of Argentina. After a few seconds, we heard him introduce himself to the consul and explain that he wanted to send him the *mate* as a gift.

Suddenly Viglione raised his voice, "… and I'm from Montevideo and you can go fuck yourself, you son of a motherfucking bitch! When I see you I'm going to smash your face in!" Then he hung up.

"Instead of thanking me," Viglione tried to explain, "that son of a bitch said he's from Buenos Aires and he doesn't drink *mate*! When I see him he better be ready!"

Undoubtedly, the *gaucho* in him came out in his angry words.

For the next week, Viglione had left us the materials and instructions to start the process of building a new barn for the sheep. Posts of a certain size had to be planted in the ground to serve as part of the structure, and all the proper measurements were outlined in his instructions.

We dug holes in the ground and planted the posts, using a weight to keep them straight. After stepping back to look at our work, we thought it looked crooked and unevenly spaced. We re-measured everything and realized that it was all correct… the crookedness was merely an optical illusion caused by the lack of walls.

When the end of the week arrived, like all previous weeks, Viglione appeared with his car full of food.

"So how's the barn coming?" he soon asked.

"Great," I answered. "Want to see it?"

"Let's go," he replied, and we headed to the field.

I already expected him to have the same impression we did when we looked at the structure. Sure enough, when we arrived, he said, "What did you do? This is all wrong!"

"Humberto," I said calmly, "don't get nervous… we thought the same thing… "

"The fucking sheep could have done a better job!" he continued, not listening.

"Measure it and you'll see."

Viglione quickly measured everything twice over and couldn't believe that it was all perfect, as ordered.

"You have to forgive me," he said, feeling guilty for his earlier outburst.

"Don't worry, Humberto. We had the same reaction when we saw it and thought we'd have to do the whole job over again. Anyway, come inside the house, we have a surprise for you."

Manuel and I had prepared a Uruguayan soup called *olla podrida*, or "rotting pot". It was a mix of everything, from vegetables and beans, to all types of meat, including chicken, beef, and pork. Viglione uncovered the pot and inhaled the delicious aroma.

"This can raise a dead man! I have stomach problems, but I'm going to eat this anyway. You both want to kill me!"

"Before you eat it, please put us in your will. That way we can continue our journey in style," I said laughing.

The next week we learned how to vaccinate sheep. Manuel would herd them through the corral and I would inject them. It was hard work. We ended up vaccinating over 400 sheep in total.

Like always, the moment had arrived for us to continue our adventure. When saying our goodbyes to Viglione, we noticed he was emotional. I thought it was weird for someone like him to get emotional during a simple farewell. With tears in his eyes he told us that we were the only ones who did not want something for nothing… we earned our money honestly through hard work. Apparently, many people have taken advantage of the kindness of the man who, to us, was more than "El Loco Viglione"… he was "El Gaucho Viglione".

# 10.

# From West to East

Our original plan was to travel to San Francisco then embark from there to Japan. We quickly disregarded this idea when we learned that Iran and Iraq were in a political conflict that could end in war. We didn't want to face another volatile situation like we did in Bolivia. So we decided to head east across the entire United States, then north to Canada. From there we could board a ship to Europe.

On a cold starry night we arrived in Reno, Nevada. The bright neon lights of the casinos were a fascinating new attraction for us.

Rows of slot machines adorned the sidewalks and our curiosity outweighed our resolve to hang on to the little money we had. Manuel dropped a quarter in the nearest machine and instantly won sixteen dollars. Since neither of us were gamblers, we decided to quit while we were ahead and look for a place to sleep.

"Tonight we'll sleep in a hotel," Manuel declared.

"Yes! Let's pretend that machine gave us a little present!" I responded happily.

Sleeping on a real bed, taking a hot shower, and eating a decent meal were three luxuries we rarely had on this journey. We almost always slept in our sleeping bags inside our tent and washed in service station bathrooms. Eating was left up to luck.

We stopped in several modest hotels but none would let us in. We realized the problem was the Indian. At the time, bikers were not well accepted, especially in the western states. Motorcycle gangs generated fear and mistrust. We were unfairly paying the price for the faults of others and had to settle for another night in the tent.

We found a rest area off the main road, pitched our tent and settled in for the night. A torrential downpour was unleashed late that night and our tent began to flood, but we kept on sleeping. We were finally awakened by the obnoxious sound of a large garbage truck. The workers just stared at us, amazed, when we got out of the tent and began to wring out our sleeping bags, gallons of water splashing to the ground. We hung them on the Indian to dry and rode out into the hills.

The hills gradually became mountains and the climate began to change as we climbed to higher altitudes. We weren't accustomed to, nor prepared for, such low temperatures. To help keep warm, we'd pick up handfuls of the free maps given out at gas stations and line our clothing with them.

Crossing into Colorado and through the Rocky Mountains, we saw snow for the first time in our lives. Neither one of us had ever had the opportunity to touch the substance so often seen in the movies. Manuel eagerly put a fistful of snow into his mouth to taste it.

"Tastes like water!" he said with a wide grin on his face.

"What did you expect," I asked, "Whisky?"

He took another handful, rolled it up into a ball, and hit me square in the face. That sparked a furious snowball war between the two of us. We were celebrating new experiences and adding one more to the many we've already had on this adventure.

We continued east and met Erik, a motorcyclist who was returning home to Denver from California. He was freezing and wearing only a light jacket, so we offered, through the use of my dictionary and hand gestures, to share some of our clothing and the use of our tent to sleep in at night. In exchange, Erik would treat us to hot meals at roadside restaurants all the way to Denver.

Once in the city, Erik gestured for us to follow him to his house. We arrived in front of two large iron gates, and

Erik took out some sort of remote control, pressed a button, and the gates parted. We were entering a huge estate like those seen only in the movies. We rolled through beautifully lighted gardens toward a spectacular mansion in the distance. Erik belonged to a very wealthy family and he had invited us to his house, offering us luxuries that are difficult to describe.

There were two houses on the expansive property... the big mansion, and a smaller house connected by a covered walkway extending from the left side of the manor. The smaller house was Erik's.

He accommodated us in one of the many bedrooms, and we took the opportunity to take hot showers... one of the luxuries we sorely missed in our travels, apart from food.

We slept peacefully, and the next morning Erik led us through the covered walkway to his parent's mansion. A very long table and a couple of fancy servants awaited us. After meeting his parents and explaining how we travelled together and helped each other, we were welcomed with a marvelous breakfast. Eating in such a luxurious environment was never in our plans, but it was certainly welcomed and accepted.

We stayed for a full week, enjoying the attention from Erik, his parents, and the serving staff. Taking pleasure in that restful oasis was also part of our adventure. The trip was full of contrasts... many times we compared the cold nights in the Andes Mountains, living with the poor natives, to our nights in Denver, in the lap of luxury with, to our eyes, probably one of the richest families in the United States.

*November 22, 1965*
*This journey is turning out to be a journey of contrasts!*

*We've learned to live with people of different cultures, education, and financial status. We are convinced that these experiences are providing us with an unparalleled education. These are things that you can't learn in school, but if you did, you wouldn't be able to absorb the knowledge like we are doing right now.*

*These stark contrasts force us to see the differences that exist in the world.*

*We're enjoying the attention here in Colorado, but tomorrow we'll continue searching for new adventures.*

Towns and cities passed by as we enjoyed the road's beautiful vistas and the local people who would approach us out of curiosity. Some were impressed by the look of the motorcycle, amazed we were travelling the world on such an old relic. Although Harley Davidson's were the most popular motorcycles in the U.S. market, we found no shortage of die hard Indian fans who professed their choice in bikes as superior.

We travelled over 3,000 miles across the U.S. from west to east. The exchange of a photo or article in a newspaper for a night of food and lodging was successful in many American cities. There were times when we wouldn't wait for the article or picture to come out in the paper and we would simply continue on our way. However, whenever we did get the chance to stay a bit longer, we would make sure to get a copy of the paper to clip out our article for our scrapbooks.

Arriving in New York City, the first thing we did was to ask around for a nearby Latino community. Hearing Manuel speak Portuguese, we were directed to Newark, New Jersey, where we found a large Portuguese community that kindly welcomed us and offered us a place to stay.

To continue our trip in a better economic condition, we decided to look for work. Newspaper after newspaper, we could not find a classified ad without a phone number, and since our English was so poor, we didn't feel comfortable calling anyone. One day we lucked out and found an ad that also contained an address. We decided to check it out, and by pure luck, the man who placed the ad was Portuguese. Thank goodness!

He offered us a janitorial job, and asked for our social security numbers. We stared at him blankly, having no idea what he was asking for. He explained it to us and gave us an address where we could attain a proper social security card. We easily obtained the cards and returned. He then gave us our assignment... meet with our new boss, Vito, an Italian man who we could communicate with in Italian.

We met Vito in an office building, where he took us in an elevator to clean the second and third floors. These floors housed chemical labs, and the hallways were so long that the walls converged to a point in the distance. Cleaning these two floors in eight hours would be impossible. As soon as Vito left us, Manuel and I began devising a plan to be able to finish the job in a reasonable time.

On our way up, we had noticed some 55 gallon drums and a large flatbed cart that we figured could be useful, provided we could fit them in the elevator.

"Did you see those huge drums and that cart near the elevator?" I asked Manuel.

"Are you thinking of getting them in the elevator?" he responded.

"Well, if we can fit the cart in the elevator with four empty drums, I think we could do the job quicker. Otherwise, I don't think we can do it in eight hours."

This reminded us of cleaning the sheep barns outside of San Francisco using the tractor. We decided to try it, and lo and behold, the cart fit! Pushing the cart with four huge drums down the long hallways allowed us to complete the task in a record four hours.

When we told Vito we completed the job, he looked at us in disbelief. He went up to inspect our work and returned astonished and happy enough to pay us for the full eight hours. The next night Vito decided to help us and we completed the job in just over three hours. Vito then agreed that we would do this every night and still get a full eight hour paycheck. He benefitted from this arrangement as well since he could go home early every night. Once again, this demonstrated how a little creativity can accomplish much more than brute force.

Now that our night job was established, we searched for a day job. This was how we planned to earn enough money to continue our voyage into Europe.

Norberto, a Brazilian friend of ours, brought us to where he worked. Chemplast Incorporated was a company that manufactured plastic products for medical labs, and they needed machine operators. Again, luck was on our side and the boss spoke Italian, which allowed me to communicate with him since Spanish and Italian are similar, and I knew enough Italian to fill in the gaps. We secured our positions and thus doubled our income, preparing for our travel into the old continent.

Working in the United States had advantages that were hard to believe. Earning a minimum wage was enough to live on, and still put some away for our trek to Europe. We were also able to buy motorcycle equipment and other necessities for the voyage.

What most drew our attention was the high quality and low prices of products. The first time I shaved, I thought the razor blades weren't working since it glided so smoothly over my face. But once I washed off the shaving cream, my face was completely smooth. I immediately mailed a pack of razor blades to my father in Uruguay, telling him that in the United States, everything was as easy as shaving with these blades.

I was earning $56.00 per week, and I was able to buy a used car for $25.00! Three pairs of underwear for only $1.00! Amazing! In a letter to my parents I told them how it was not even worth washing them!

The American way of life was very different from any other country we had visited. Unemployment was under 3% and jobs were plentiful. Items of necessity were very affordable and salaries were good. This is what we called a good standard of living.

We would work all week, then explore on the weekends. We were impressed with the engineering of the bridges and tunnels that took us from New Jersey to Manhattan. We were almost afraid of taking either of the two tunnels that passed under the Hudson River and deposited us in the city.

If Buenos Aires impressed us as the capital of South America, New York City could be considered the capital of the entire continent. This great metropolis had everything. People of different races could be seen everywhere, and various cultures mixed and mingled together. Chinatown, Harlem, Spanish Harlem, Brooklyn, The Bronx, 42nd Street, Broadway, Fifth Avenue, Central Park... time was short to take in all the attractions New York had to offer. Weekends in the city were inevitable. Attending concerts in Central Park was something we enjoyed and would cost us very little.

One night we were in Greenwich Village, the hippie neighborhood. We made friends with a couple of them and they invited us to stay the night in their apartment and explore more of the city the next day. Entering their home we noticed that many hippies were living there, men and women, all sharing rooms together.

Marijuana was their drug of choice and they could not believe that we, who came from South America where a lot of it was grown, would not join them in smoking it.

They became fascinated with our voyage and would sit for hours listening to our stories, aided by hand signals and a dictionary. All in all, they were very peaceful and friendly people.

# 11.

# Wanted by the FBI

It was a beautiful autumn night in New Jersey, perfect for enjoying the wind in my face and letting my thoughts and memories fly in the freedom of the ride. Guiding my old Indian on a well-travelled road towards the beach, I wondered to myself why Manuel and I, being such good friends, would always go our separate ways every time we reached a new destination.

We were both very different, but we were the best of friends. We never argued, even under the harshest of circumstances. We survived gunfire during the Bolivian Revolution, a serious accident in Panama, suffered extreme cold, heat, and hunger. We crossed countries, rivers, mountains, and deserts together, and we never once disagreed or argued about anything. Yet every time we arrived at major destinations along our path, we'd separate without really understanding why.

The fresh air seemed to etch these thoughts into my mind, and I felt a little guilty for having turned down Manuel's invitation to go to Manhattan that night with some of his friends.

"Let's go, Flaco!" he had insisted. "We'll see the great city, drink a little, and have some fun!"

For a brief moment, I had almost agreed to go just so that I would not say "no" to him one more time. But the crisp autumn night offered me such peace that I couldn't bring myself to go partying in the city.

"You don't know what you're missing!' Manuel teased as he entered the car of one of his friends. We waved to each other and parted ways once again.

I arrived at the coast where I gazed at a clear night sky filled with millions of tiny stars twinkling as if sending messages to each other. I parked my motorcycle and sat on the sand, enjoying the solitude and the cosmic spectacle that transmitted such peace. These were moments of mental reflection, inspiration, and great tranquility. Nothing could recharge my adventurous spirit more than these special moments, which were, incredibly, free.

When I returned to our apartment, it was already early morning, and Manuel had not yet returned from his night out. I was later awakened by a timid knock on the door.

Opening the door, I found one of my neighbors, who looked rather worried. Nervously, she said, "Last night two very large *gringos* came looking for you. They said they were from the FBI and they had a picture of you and your friend. They asked if I had seen you."

At that moment, I thought of Manuel, who had not come home last night and whose bed was still empty. Had something happened to him? If the FBI had our pictures and was looking for us, something was very wrong.

The next morning, the uncertainty, my common sense, and my clean conscience obligated me to present myself to a local police station to ask why we were wanted. Norberto, whose English was better than mine, accompanied me, and we explained everything to the officer in charge. The officer made several phone calls and told us to sit and wait.

About 45 minutes later, two very large men walked in through the doors of the police station, identifying themselves as FBI agents, and speaking almost perfect Spanish.

We were taken to a private room where the two men asked for our names and other personal information as they diligently scribbled in their little notepads. They showed us a picture of me and Manuel on the bike. It was a copy of the cards we would hand out as souvenirs of our trip. They had enlarged and retouched the picture so our faces were the central focus.

I explained that Manuel and I were on a motorcycle trip, and that these cards were handed out as souvenirs to those we would meet along the way. They then urged me to tell them what I had done the night before. I detailed my ride to the beach and even told them of some of the thoughts I had during my peaceful night.

"Were you accompanied by anyone or did anyone see you?" the larger of the two asked in a very commanding voice.

"No," I responded without hesitation. "No one accompanied me. But Manuel and some of his friends saw me right before I took off for the beach and they headed for New York."

"Anyone else see you?" the smaller man asked.

"Well, I don't know. I don't think so," I answered.

I didn't have to be a psychic to realize what they were after. Something had happened the night before with Manuel and his friends, and they wanted to know if I was involved in any way.

After an exhaustive interrogation, they explained to me and Norberto that the car that Manuel was in the previous night had been involved in a fatal hit and run of two motorists that were changing a tire on the side of the highway between New York and New Jersey. Apparently frightened of what had occurred Manuel and his friends had abandoned the car and ran. The FBI was obviously looking for all those involved, and one of those was Manuel.

The investigation had led them to me as a suspect since they had figured out that Manuel and I were travelling companions. They had questioned me very insistently, and I had no alibi and could not otherwise prove that I was not involved.

"You need to accompany us to Jersey City," the larger man stated.

I figured I had nothing to fear since my conscience was clean having truly not been involved in the incident, but two things worried me. One was Manuel and the trouble he was in, and the other was how I was going to prove my innocence.

We got into a Cadillac, and I thought to myself that these two huge agents wouldn't have fit into any other car. The car ride was silent, and we soon arrived at the Jersey City prison. When I saw the huge walls and all the guards, I asked myself if I'd ever be able to escape. I had never been to a prison before, not even to visit, and I now had no idea if I'd ever leave.

So many wild thoughts were crossing my mind that I no longer trusted the outcome of this whole affair, regardless of my innocence. I could no longer think clearly. I was in a country that was not mine, my English wasn't good enough to be able to express my thoughts clearly, and I was practically being accused of a heinous crime. I knew that in the United States, a man is innocent until proven guilty, but how would this play out if I could not express my innocence clearly enough?

We walked through a maze of corridors and doors until we reached a room with a large rectangular table surrounded by chairs. They told us to sit down, and then they left us alone for over an hour. Norberto and I talked about everything that had happened. At one point in our conversation, I gave him a subtle wink... I can't remember exactly why... and afterwards, when I realized there were probably hidden cameras in the room, I kept winking randomly, faking a nervous tic.

Of course, we were being filmed and recorded as part of the investigation. They left us alone in that room to compare our "private" conversation with the facts we had given them in the earlier interrogations.

The door opened and a handcuffed man was led in… one of Manuel's friends who had accompanied him in the car the previous night. I later found out that this man was the driver.

They sat him down at the opposite end of the table, and asked him in a loud voice, "Do you know this man?" as they pointed to me.

I never felt more uncomfortable in my entire life. Throughout our adventure, I had suffered through difficult times, but all of it was under my control. Now, everything depended on this man telling the truth. I realized that my freedom was in the hands of a stranger who was himself accused of killing a man.

My knees went weak under the table, and I tried to mentally transmit a positive attitude to the man who held my future in his next words.

"Yes, I know him," he responded dryly. "He is travelling around the world on a motorcycle with one of my friends."

A cold sweat enveloped my entire body as I listened to the words coming from his mouth with the cadence of a condemned man.

"Was this man in the car you were driving… the car you abandoned after running over and killing two innocent people?" the large man yelled.

"No. He was not with us that night," he answered.

I held back a huge sigh of relief having heard his declaration that proved my innocence. The question was asked over and over, and each time he answered the same way.

The prisoner was then escorted roughly out of the room, and I quickly realized they weren't finished with me when they brought in another handcuffed man… one I had seen in the car on the night of the fatal accident. I knew him as the car's owner.

The questions were the same as before, and they were screamed more than asked. Luckily the answers were all in my favor and I was finally absolved of all suspicion.

The two FBI agents, Frank and John, then kindly invited me and Norberto to a nice dinner, apologizing for the grueling interviews and explaining how difficult their jobs are.

Arriving back in our apartment on Adams Street, I found a note that had been slipped under the door. It was in Manuel's handwriting. He was asking for me to bring his clothes to an address in Manhattan.

The next day I noticed that I was being followed. There was someone behind me at all times… several men, in fact, as they seemed to be taking turns. Taking Manuel his clothes would be like delivering him to the police. I knew the only mistake Manuel made was fleeing the scene of the accident. I also knew that he was not driving the car, and most of all, I knew that he was a good man in a bad situation.

I decided to find a way to get Manuel his clothes. This was not about the clothes, but about giving my friend a final hug as he could no longer be a part of this adventure. I also wanted to know what he was planning to do as he was now a wanted man.

Winter was coming and the days were getting progressively colder. I decided to go to Manhattan and somehow evade those following me. I got on my Indian and immediately spied two men rushing to get into their car behind me, determined not to lose me.

I took Ferry Street in Newark and turned right on Broad Street, hardly slowing, dodging cars the whole way. With several speedy zigzags I lost sight of my persecutors.

I quickly dismounted the bike and left it on a side street and turned my reversible jacket inside-out, changing its color. From there I went to a bus stop and took the bus to Penn Station, where I then boarded another bus bound for Manhattan. The proverbial mouse has eluded the cat.

Once I arrived in the city, I found the address and finally met up with Manuel, who tried to explain what I already knew… he was innocent but fled the scene in fear.

Luckily, Manuel had connections that managed to get him a passport under a different name so he could return to Brazil. We hugged strongly, and with tear-filled eyes we wished each other luck and parted ways. I would continue this journey alone, hoping to one day see him again, perhaps when we were older, and reminisce about our youthful adventure.

I was constantly being followed by the FBI, no doubt still searching for Manuel and the others involved in the hit and run. With all this going on, plus work and little rest, I hadn't written in my journal in a while. Finally, on December 13th, I wrote:

*December 13, 1965*

*I took a big risk in eluding the FBI and bringing Manuel his suitcase. Standing with him in a building in Manhattan, I looked out the window and saw police cars below. I thought for sure I had been followed.*

*Manuel had attained new papers and would be leaving for Rio de Janeiro tomorrow. After saying our goodbyes, I feared leaving the building, thinking I'd be stopped by the cops. I took a deep breath, left the building and walked right by them. They totally ignored me! What a relief!*

Although I was cleared of all wrong-doing, I knew that I'd be vigilantly followed as they searched for Manuel. I was still employed at Chemplast, and since I had a good rapport with my boss, I managed to get my friend Luis a job there.

I met Luis Nievas in Uruguay on the day we were interviewed on TV, just a few days before we started our journey. Months later, Luis had come to the United States and we reconnected in Newark, New Jersey.

One sunny winter day I was with Luis and as we climbed onto my Indian, a car pulled up and stopped us. Three large men got out and identified themselves as policemen, flashing their badges. They had apparently mistaken Luis for Manuel, so they took us in.

After they realized their mistake, they said we were free to go, but that we'd have to come back the next day for the Indian since they had removed the distributor rotor to prevent any possibility of escape. Indignant, I told them that this was an outrage, and that their methods were bordering on harassment. I left with my motorcycle that very night.

*December 23, 1965*
*Today I experienced an uncommon indignation when Luis and I were detained by local police. I realized that even though things had been cleared up with the FBI, the word had not been disseminated down the ranks to other law enforcement agencies. I can't understand why this information has not been transmitted, and I fear that I'll be stopped and questioned everywhere I go in the United States.*

*I think what bothers me more is that they disabled my Indian... my faithful companion for so many miles. My old bike has an almost human personality to me and I truly feel pain that she has been violated.*

# 12.

# To Europe

Christmas came just like any other day. I was sad that I would be travelling alone from this point on. Manuel and I never argued about anything. With everything we've been through, I would miss him terribly.

Parked outside on Adams Street, the Indian suffered cold and snowy days. Every morning I would dig her out to be able to get to work, and every night I'd return her to the same spot. Working was how I was earning enough money to continue on to Canada, then to Europe.

I thought to wait out the bad weather before continuing my adventure, but time was short. The day finally came when I decided to leave. I had to say my goodbyes to my friends and coworkers, and I decided to tell them the truth of my journey, something I was afraid to tell them about earlier for fear of being let go. Ralph, my boss, was surprised but totally understood and told me that if I ever returned to the United States, I would have a job and that the company could even help pay for continuing education, and help me obtain my immigrant visa. That told me that they were happy with my work and that the changes I had implemented there had increased production in a significant and noticeable way.

Winter was at its peak and I had a ticket to embark from Saint John's, Canada to Dublin, Ireland. This time I was prepared, wearing long underwear, gloves and a warm overcoat. The Indian had been outfitted with a new windshield and special leg covers that protected me even more from the cold.

It was the 12th of February and the trip north began with an impressive snowstorm. I had to get to Saint John's in three days or I'd miss the boat.

I had to let out some air from my tires to increase the surface area and improve the tire's grip on the snowy roads. Every town I entered greeted me with local patrolmen stopping me to ask why I was riding in such a bad snowstorm.

Near Boston, I was signaled to stop by a man in a pickup truck, apparently also curious as to why I would be out on a motorcycle in a blizzard. I tried to explain to him, in my broken English, all about my trip. He invited me to dinner that night and later gave me the only thing I was missing... a ski mask. He also gave me a wool sweater containing a drawing of a caveman with a fig leaf covering his private parts, and the phrase "Be Nice To Me... I Am Rich" printed on the front.

On those cold nights I would clear the snow off the ground with a small army shovel, lay out my sleeping bag, and cover it with my tent. The cold was so intense that I would climb into my sleeping bag without removing my clothes, including my boots. The sleeping bag, designed by the American Army and heavily quilted with down, would trap my body heat, and in about five minutes the temperature would start to rise and I'd have to take off my clothes. This is how the Indian and I would pass the cold, starry nights.

Arriving in Saint John's, a reporter approached me to do a story about my hard adventure. In exchange I asked for two nights in a hotel with dinner and breakfast included. He agreed and led me to a fancy hotel in the city. He ended up writing one of the best accounts of the journey. It began, "He's not an animal... he's not Superman... he's simply a young Uruguayan travelling around the world on his old Indian Chief motorcycle... "

After two nights of rest, I went to the port of Saint John's, the final leg of my North American travels, and where I would embark to Ireland. I had my ticket paid for, but I had to negotiate the Indian's passage.

"For the motorcycle, do you charge by weight or by size?" I asked the man on duty.

"By size," he responded.

"Ahh," I said, thinking.

I immediately grabbed some tools and started to take apart my bike. I removed the large box that held all my belongings and took that with me as my luggage. I removed the windshield and tied it to the Indian's side. I loosened the handlebars and tilted them down. I even removed air from the tires. With all these modifications, I was able to save $70, which represented many meals or gallons of gasoline in Europe.

The boat was known as Torr Head, a cargo and passenger vessel flying the Norwegian flag. It was a rather large boat but only had room for 12 passengers, though on this trip it carried only two.

The Indian was deposited in the cargo bay and I planned to spend a few days resting, reading, and eating as much as I could. I was alone, and in my loneliness I would write about my recent adventures and read them out loud.

The other passenger was a Canadian professor who planned to tour Europe. The Torr Head was not without its luxuries. We would eat dinner with the captain every night. The first night, the crew offered up a grand feast and I was served a large, succulent looking steak. Beef, besides being my favorite meat, was also rarely eaten during my trip because of the price. When I saw that plate, my eyes could hardly believe what they were seeing. When the waiter began pouring apple sauce all over the steak, I began to cry out, "Noooo!" But it was too late. I did my best to scrape the apple sauce off the beautiful steak, and I pleaded that next time they serve beef to skip the sauce.

On the Torr Head, the conversations were always in English, and though I mostly couldn't understand a thing, these conversations were helping me practice the difficult English language.

A huge storm hit on the second day that lasted the rest of the trip. At night I would sleep fastened to my bed with belts that were made specifically for that purpose. The waves were so huge that the porthole in my cabin was permanently under water. After five more days, the storm finally subsided as we were nearing the Irish coast.

Once in port, the Torr Head was boarded by Irish immigration officers to interview the two passengers, me and the professor.

The professor apparently did not pass scrutiny and was not allowed to disembark. When it was my turn, I began to explain how I was riding my motorcycle around the world, and after presenting my papers, the big question was asked.

"You need money to tour Europe. How much money do you have?"

At this point in time, I was very experienced in successful border crossings. With confidence I pulled out my wallet, filled with money I had earned in the United States, and at the same time I opened my jacket and showed them my caveman sweater with the "Be Nice To Me… I Am Rich" slogan. They stamped my passport with a smile and both me and my Indian were granted entry into Ireland.

# 13.

## Touring Europe

The Indian was hoisted off the boat with a crane that was attached to the pavement in the port of Dublin. There we were, just me and my faithful companion, alone on another continent, ready to start a new adventure.

I immediately began putting my bike back together... the windshield was reattached, the luggage put back in its place, and I filled the tires with air. I had to work hard to save a few dollars, but in the end it was worth it.

After seven days of not feeling solid ground, I left the port in an almost euphoric state, excited to know that my adventure in the Old World was about to begin.

I toured the plazas and monuments of that first European city and I felt a renewed sense of freedom. I didn't have to answer to anyone and I, being prone to spur of the moment decisions, changed course with frequency. Even when following a plan, I would often abandon it and find myself making a new plan, never really knowing where my next decision would take me.

Every so often I would write in my journal...

*February 26, 1966*
*I disembarked in Ireland. Here, things are a little more difficult. The only way to communicate with anyone is in English... there doesn't seem to be anyone here that speaks Spanish, or any other romance language that is easier for me to understand. Another weird thing is that they drive on the left side of the road here, which I am finding very difficult to get used to. I have the tendency to drive on the right side and keep finding myself going against the flow of traffic.*

Whenever I would arrive in a new city, I had to find a cheap place to sleep. In the outskirts of a city it was always easier since I could simply pitch my tent anywhere, but Dublin was not what you would call rural.

I stopped a taxi driver and asked him in my broken English, "Where can I find a cheap room in Dublin?"

"Well, you could go to the Salvation Army. It's very affordable," he replied.

I didn't like the idea, but when he told me the prices, I changed my mind and arrived at the Salvation Army. It cost 25 cents for a plate of food, and 50 cents to sleep for the night... truly affordable.

I immediately realized that in Europe, everything was different than in the United States. There was no work available, and begging was out of the question. The only way to survive was to stretch the money I brought with me as far as I could.

Dublin seemed to me like a place with a strong cultural tradition. I almost compared it to Montevideo, with its small area and population. Ireland felt like an underdeveloped country, where the people were satisfied sitting in a bar, chatting about how to fix the world. Yes... Dublin was very much like Montevideo.

I was very impressed with my visit to Malahide Castle, which had belonged to the Talbot family since 1185. Dublin was the city of castles... at least that's how it seemed to me. The castles of Dublin, Drimnagh, Dalkey, and Ardgillan were proof of that. These were historic constructions, from their cathedrals to the family living quarters.

I figured that Europe had so much to offer that I would lose myself in its history and enjoy the unparalleled art of the ages. Europe would be the dessert after a difficult journey, and perhaps even the espresso coffee that would help me digest my entire adventure.

My Indian and I stayed in Ireland for a few days, and then took a ferry boat to the port of Liverpool, England. We arrived in Liverpool on a cloudy day, which seemed very common in England. I looked for and found another Salvation Army, which, truth be told, I had enjoyed in Ireland. To this day, whenever I see someone collecting money for the Salvation Army, I am happy to donate.

I briefly toured Manchester and Birmingham on my way to London. In these old European cities, even the smells seemed ancient. I could tell why this was called The Old World.

The architecture and art were fascinating and abundant. This was truly a different way to travel, from city to city, soaking up the history and the culture, without ever crossing large expanses of empty wilderness.

London was also very impressive, from Buckingham Palace and the Royal Guard, to the large plazas filled with people... it all left me with a distinct European impression that I had not seen or felt in all of modern America. Much of the United States had been built by the English and Irish, but the country had converted itself into a country of drive and consumption, where people thought and lived differently. Americans were not relegated in history, but rather embraced technology and hard work, which elevated their economic status to the point where most Americans lived comfortably.

My tour of London was not extensive, but I appreciated this historical and famous city. I could not afford to travel Europe like most people, so I started following the double-decker buses full of tourists, and would join their excursions from afar and for free. I followed them throughout the city and was satisfied with simply watching them cruise the Thames, and viewing the churches and monuments from the outside only since I did not want to spend money on the entrance fee.

Like always, I looked for the consulate for the next country I would be visiting so I could obtain a travel visa. While visiting the French consulate, I saw two guys dressed in the stereotypical biker uniform: blue jeans, black boots, leather jacket, and white t-shirt. Curiosity got the better of me and I initiated a conversation.

"What are you doing in the French consulate?" I asked in my slowly improving English.

"We're looking to attain a travel visa into France," one of them said in a thick English accent. "Ken here is a U.S. citizen and needs one," he continued, pointing at his partner.

"We're planning a motorcycle excursion to Australia."

"I'm also travelling by motorcycle," I answered.

"Really? What kind of bike are you riding?" the second guy asked in his obvious American accent.

"A 1947 Indian Chief," I responded, watching their astonished expressions.

"1947?" they asked in unison.

"Yes, and I've already travelled through the three Americas and Ireland. My plan is to now tour Europe," I explained to my two new friends. "What kind of motorcycle are you taking to Australia?" I asked.

"It's a BSA 650 with a sidecar," the Englishman answered.

They finally introduced themselves as Roger and Ken, and thus began a friendship of three adventurers, each from a different country.

They were both professional scuba divers, and were previously under contract by a wealthy businessman to dive for sunken treasure. He always hired the best divers in the world, and Roger and Ken certainly fit that description. They managed to find the treasure and were paid very well, so they felt they deserved a vacation.

Roger invited me to stay for a few days in his house in Ramsgate, outside of London, and then travel with them to Paris. Since I had only spent a few days in London, I accepted his invitation.

*March 1, 1966*

*I'm enjoying my time at Roger's house with his close family, telling stories of my adventures, and practicing my English. We'll be travelling to France together.*

*Today they installed the sidecar on their B.S.A. and filled it with their belongings. In my opinion, the motorcycle is too small to be pulling such a big load, but I didn't say anything. I don't want to offend my new friends.*

*I hope we leave soon because I think I'm falling for Roger's sister.*

We left one cloudy morning and I'll never forget the vision of Roger's mother waving goodbye to her son. It brought back memories of my parent's farewell to me at the start of my voyage with Manuel. This farewell managed to moisten my eyes.

We cruised on the English asphalt, always on the left side of the road. My old Indian and I were in no hurry, travelling leisurely and soaking in the vistas. Roger's BSA, with its over-packed sidecar, was always in front of us, rushing ahead as if Roger wanted to reach Paris in the next two minutes.

Stopping for coffee, I delicately brought up the fact that I felt their motorcycle was packed too heavily. I also explained that I was in no rush and that I preferred to ride at a pace where I could enjoy the landscapes.

We reached the port of Dover and we quickly bought ferry tickets to cross the English Channel to the port of Calais, France. It was past noon when we reached the other side. We stopped for a quick bite before continuing on to the City of Lights. It was dusk by the time we reached Paris.

The word that best describes Paris is "majestic". The streets were full of life, impressively illuminated by the glow of a million colors and faces. Now I began to see the Old World from a unique perspective.

The theaters, buildings, the Champs-Élysées , the Arc de Triomphe, the Eiffel Tower… I wanted to see it all that very night as I rode from street to street with unparalleled enthusiasm.

We checked in to a campground that Ken knew of in the city, planning to spend several days exploring the area. After setting up camp, I noticed that Roger and Ken were preoccupied with their motorcycle. They said the motor was making a weird noise. Having mechanical experience, I figured I'd help out my new friends.

I placed the tip of a screwdriver directly on the motor and held the handle to my ear, using it as a stethoscope to amplify the sound. I could immediately tell that there was probably a problem in one of the cranks. The extra weight on the bike, as well as running it at high speeds, certainly contributed to the problem, and the only way to repair it would be to disassemble the entire engine.

Roger and Ken did not have any spare parts, tools, or knowledge to do the job, and although I offered my help, they decided that it would be better for them to return home and have the engine repaired in England.

That night, I retired to my tent to get some sleep. My two travelling companions decided to go out on the town to enjoy at least one night in Paris before heading home. About four hours later I heard these two returning to camp, with

Roger practically dragging the drunken Ken along. I pretended I was asleep so I wouldn't get dragged into their heated, and most likely alcohol fueled, discussion.

The next morning, I found them in the campground's bathroom, Roger still arguing with his obviously still not fully recovered friend. I couldn't even begin to understand what they were arguing about.

*March 5, 1966*

*Last night I noticed my two new friends were behaving oddly. I figured if someone had asked me which of the two would have returned to camp drunk, I would have said Roger without thinking twice about it, mostly because he's British. I was ashamed, not because I was wrong, but because I had immediately condemned one man because of his nationality alone.*

*When I found the two of them in the bathroom, they were tense and indifferent. I think of Manuel, of all we have suffered through together, and I feel good that we have never had such disagreements.*

*Roger and Ken have only been travelling together for one day, and it's obvious things aren't going well. I believe that's why Roger suggested taking the bike back to England... to cut the trip short and possibly to postpone the voyage to Australia indefinitely.*

Later, Roger and Ken informed me that they were indeed heading back to England. They loaded the BSA, sidecar and all, onto a truck, and bid me farewell, leaving me and my Indian alone to plan new adventures.

I followed a tourist excursion that began at the campground and promised to show all of Paris in less than four hours. Following them, I toured the Champs-Élysées, the Arc de Triomphe, the Eiffel Tower, the Trocadéro, the Notre Dame Cathedral, Concorde Square, and other points of interest. Naturally, I had to repeat the tour a few times since I would inevitably stay in one location longer than the tour allowed. My Indian and I stayed in Paris for several days, sightseeing by day and camping at night.

One brisk and sunny morning, I left the City of Lights, bound for Belgium, hoping to reach Brussels that same day. The European roads were narrow but in good condition. In France and Belgium people drove on the right side of the road, making it much more comfortable for me than in Ireland or England. The sky was darkening by the time I reached Brussels.

I asked a boy working a newspaper stand, in my already improving but still broken English, where I could find inexpensive lodging. He recommended a youth hostel nearby, stating that although the place wasn't very nice, it was certainly easy on the pocketbook. I headed there without a second thought.

While registering at the hostel, I met Albert, a Danish guy dressed in a leather jacket lined with fleece, like I saw in Canada. He was also travelling by motorcycle, and we quickly became friends.

I removed my belongings from the box attached to the Indian, and went to the room I was assigned to. It was an enormous room with well over 100 beds. The smells were certainly not agreeable, but I figured that after a good shower I'd get some rest. To my surprise, there was only hot water one day a week, and this was not that day. I took a freezing cold shower, and within minutes, Albert and I were already planning on finding a different place to stay the next day.

At seven in the morning, we left that grim and dirty place on the hunt for a more agreeable place to set up camp. Since Albert could communicate well with the locals, he quickly found out about a campground at the border of the city. After a quick coffee break, we headed straight there. We found it easily and made arrangements to pitch our tents there for a few days while we toured Brussels.

*March 10, 1966*
*I met a fellow biker named Albert. He's 26, like me, and plans to go from Belgium to France, Switzerland, then Italy, where he has a Chilean friend who's expecting him. From here, I plan to travel to the Netherlands, Germany, Switzerland, and then Italy, where Albert and I promised to reconnect in 30 days in the Piazza del Popolo in Rome.*

*We'll stay in Brussels for three days where we'll explore the city together.*

Brussels, the bi-lingual capital city, was a city of contrasts. In the streets you could hear a lot of German and French, which seemed the two most common languages. Digging a little deeper you might find some English speakers as well.

The architecture also displayed the same contrasts as the spoken language, offering vastly different styles in close proximity.

The departure point for tourists is the Grand Place, where roads burst out like arteries leading to every point of interest in the city. From there, the four of us, me and my Indian,

Albert and his trusty companion, set out to ride along the streets and take in the surroundings.

I showed Albert my method of following planned excursions from a distance, and we enjoyed Brussels in a way that had Albert marveling at the plan's simplicity and economy.

Like always, the time came to say our goodbyes. When two people are doing similar uncommon things, such as travelling the world on motorcycles, a certain camaraderie and bond exists between them. With a hug like we've been life-long friends, we parted ways.

The old Indian rolled on towards the Netherlands when a set of fierce dark clouds erupted into a downpour. I stopped to put on my raincoat, then continued on as if nothing had happened. The bad weather did not concern me. It certainly wasn't comfortable to ride in the rain, but this was now simply one of the variables that I had become accustomed to on such a journey as this. The rain continued as I arrived in Amsterdam.

Traversing a central street I noticed that all the businesses had signs written in Spanish. I parked my bike and walked into a store to see if I could be directed to a cheap hotel. They told me, in perfect Spanish, that I was in the Latino section of town. I joked that I took a wrong turn and must be in Spain.

Although the rain had subsided a bit, the streets were slick and dangerous with the mixture of rain water and motor oil leaked from the many cars that travel the city streets. I confidently kick started my Indian and headed to the recommended motel, a small place owned by Spaniards. From there I could branch out and get to know the city and its surroundings.

Days passed and the rain continued relentlessly, forcing me to reluctantly decide to continue on to Germany. Due to the bad weather I was not able to experience Amsterdam how I would have liked. Known as the "Venice of the North" for its many canals, I could see that this city offered many attractions. The parks and architecture slightly more modern than that of Ireland, England, France and Belgium were the only things I got to appreciate during my brief stay.

Winter had returned and riding was not so much fun in the middle of a cold Northern Europe. The Dutch countryside was filled with cows and windmills, just like I had seen on many travel brochures. Despite the bad weather, I still enjoyed myself and felt like Don Quixote riding my own *Rocinante*, my old Indian Chief.

I left Amsterdam from the south, following the Belgian border until I crossed into Germany through the customs station at Aachen. Bonn was nearby and I stopped there for the night. The next day I pointed my bike south once again toward the Swiss border. The roads were well maintained but always winding due to the many mountains they traversed. These very mountains gave the German towns the aura of a beautiful old-fashioned postcard. There were a few moments when I felt the caress of a snowflake or two on my face, melting before it reached the ground.

I headed to Frankfurt, the famous German city rife with history. Divided by the Main River, Frankfurt appeared to me to be very technologically and industrially advanced. I could tell this was an important city, with all the conveniences and inconveniences of any major metropolis. I befriended a group of young motorcyclists interested in learning more about my voyage. We drank room temperature German beer, which was very different from the ice cold beer from the Americas that I was used to.

Between hand signals and an English dictionary I was able to tell the tale of my adventure with my old Indian, which fascinated the folks in the land of BMW's. I had the opportunity to stay in Frankfurt for a few days in my new friend Helmut's house. Helmut guided me to several important landmarks in the city, through the cold and snow. Every night we'd end up drinking beer and chatting in a strange mix of languages. After a few days I was back on my own and headed south.

*March 20, 1966*
   *Winter seems endless. It's hard to travel like a rich man on a poor man's plan, and I can't afford the luxury of waiting out the weather.*
   *I decided to continue on to Switzerland knowing that it's snowing there and I'm afraid they'll close the roads to Italy, leaving me to wait out the European winter, which I am not enjoying one bit.*

I entered Switzerland in a snow storm. I again had to remove some air from the tires for better traction on the slippery roadways.

While approaching the city of Berne, a poster advertising a mountainside campground caught my attention. Arriving there moments later, I met with the campground administrator, an older woman whose features prominently displayed the unrelenting tracks of time. I tried to speak with her but she couldn't understand a word I was saying. English, Spanish, Portuguese, Italian... no language I tried broke through the communication gap.

After several unsuccessful minutes of trying to understand me, the woman left for a nearby trailer and returned with an old man, who could presumably act as a translator.

"Hello," he said in perfect Spanish, with an authentic pure-bred accent. "Do you speak Spanish?"

"Of course, it's my language," I replied.

"I'm from Spain but I've been working here in Switzerland for many years," he explained.

"Well, I'm glad you're here, then, since I can't seem to communicate with the administrator... and I tried in several languages."

"What do you need?"

"I just need a place to set up my tent and spend the night," I replied simply.

"Isn't it a little cold to sleep in a tent?"

"I'm used to it, and I have decent gear. The problem is I have very little money." I went on to describe my journey so far while the man translated.

The woman responded with something that sounded favorable.

"She said you can stay in one of the cabins, which will be much more comfortable than a tent," he told me happily. "You can also keep the motorcycle in the tool shed," he added.

Apparently, the woman was fascinated with my story and was kind enough to let me use a cabin, already being heated by a wood burning stove. I put the Indian in the nearby tool shed and carried my gear to the cabin, which to me was downright palatial. After a few minutes, the woman showed up with a tray of food and a mug of hot chocolate. I could tell she was intrigued by my journey, or at least by the manner in which I was undergoing it.

*March 22, 1966*

*This is a paradise surrounded by snow. I arrived at a campground in Berne last night and found my host to be a very friendly old woman who let me stay in a cabin for a ridiculously low price. I'm now sitting at the foot of the wood stove, a couple of dry logs burning within, and I feel like a king.*

*Last night, after settling in, my host brought me a piece of cake and a cup of hot chocolate, which restored the life in me that had been slowly draining by the four days of torrential downpours and accumulated snow on the roads.*

*There are good people in the world, and I feel compelled to write this down so I won't forget it tomorrow… or ever.*

*I'll stay another day here, enjoying the hospitality, and recharging for the rest of my trip. Tomorrow I plan to head to Italy since it's snowing hard and I'm afraid they'll close the borders.*

While preparing to head out for Italy, the translator came up to me looking worried. He told me that there was only one road to Italy left open… the Great Saint Bernard Pass.

After studying the map, I headed for the Italian border. On the way I discovered a small, picturesque restaurant. I decided to stop and get something warm to battle the intense cold of the Swiss Alps.

Looking around, I noticed that due to the amount of snow, many people were arriving on skis.

I parked my Indian next to a BMW motorcycle that looked fully loaded for long distance travel. A moment later, the owner came out, speaking to me in English. He was asking me all sorts of questions about how to ride in the snow. Proudly, I showed him the Indian's tires, explaining the advantages of a wider base. I also explained how I had let out some air from each tire to increase their surface area and provide better traction in the snow.

Excited with what he had learned, the man let out air from each tire, leaving them both rather flat, and rode off to the South. I watched him leave, a bit concerned.

I entered the restaurant and remained inside for over half an hour, not wanting to leave the comfort of a warm wood stove. When I finally left, I climbed onto my Indian, repeated the routine to start its potent motor, and headed off toward the Great Saint Bernard Pass.

I rode past spectacular vistas, perfectly framed by snow covered mountains, worthy of being immortalized in postcards or paintings. After a few more miles, I spotted the back of the BMW, timidly advancing on the snowy road. I was already used to riding in the snow, and the Indian, with its wide tires, had become a respectable snow tracker. I easily passed the BMW, giving a friendly wave to its rider. He contented himself with a head nod my way, not wanting to let go of the handlebars.

Arriving at the Great Saint Bernard Pass, I presented my documents to the curious customs official, and finally entered Italy. My plan was to reach Turin, where an old friend from my racing days now lived. Thomas Marello was the owner of a motorcycle garage in Uruguay, but decided to return to his homeland of Italy around the same time I had embarked on my long journey. He had given me his address in Turin in case I ever travelled to his country.

It was nighttime by the time I reached Turin. I had to make several stops asking for directions before I finally found his address. I felt fairly comfortable with the Italian I had learned from Don Vero. The tall, modern building was located in a nice area of the city.

Parking in front of the building, I quickly entered the lobby and found a list of everyone who lived there. I scanned the list and found Thomas Marello, and headed for his apartment. Knocking on his door resulted in no answer. A neighbor told me Thomas owned a restaurant and worked nights. She gave me directions.

How could Marello own a restaurant? Ever since I've known him, he's been working on motorcycles, and I couldn't imagine him doing anything else. I started my bike and navigated through the streets of Turin, following the directions I was given. It wasn't far and I arrived earlier than I expected.

Without entering the restaurant, I revved the Indian's motor a few times, and a few seconds later Marello came running outside and gave me a big hug. He said that by the sound of it, an Indian had arrived in Turin, and it couldn't be anyone other than me riding her.

"Look at you! You're crazy!" he said over and over, not believing his eyes.

"How the hell are you, old friend?" I asked.

"Tell me! Tell me!" he repeated excitedly.

"If I tell you the whole story now, we'll die here!" I told him.

"Fuck, man! You are crazy!" he repeated.

"What about you? You traded in steel for utensils? Who's the crazy one?"

"I got too old to keep riding," he explained.

"You remember our racing days?" I asked.

"How could I forget? Come on. Come inside, let's eat."

"Eat? What is that? I don't remember," I joked.

"Seriously, Flaco. You're looking mighty thin. Come inside."

We entered his restaurant and I greeted Marello's wife, who was also surprised to see me again. We talked all night long, past closing time. Marello and his wife left in a car, and I followed closely on my Indian.

They had invited me to stay with them during my time in Turin. There was so much to catch up on that we finally went to sleep after the sun had come up.

The next afternoon we went to the basement of the building, where every apartment had its own wine cellar for owners to make or store their acquired wines. Marello was of the making type, and I had arrived during the time when the wine needed to be transferred from barrels to bottles. I promised to give him a hand with this process, and we took several empty bottles down with us to the cellar to get started.

Of course, it was logical for us to try the wine that, according to Marello, was made with very high quality harvest grapes. Once we finished filling the bottles, and ourselves, our legs felt like rubber. We couldn't even stand up from our drunken stupor. We stumbled our way back up to the apartment and slept for a long while. Our friendship was one of reminiscing good times, and enjoying our memories.

Nearly a week had passed, and I had toured through most of Turin, my old friend as my tour guide. The day came when I said goodbye to Marello and his wife and headed to the south of Italy.

While riding through the central streets of Turin, I thought to myself that I would need to have my parents send more money to a bank in Rome for me. The little money I did currently have would likely not last until Rome, so I had to find a way to remedy the immediate problem.

I figured that if I could find a pawn shop, I could leave a few items in exchange for some money, and I'd pick them back up on my return through Turin, then circle around to the coast of the Mediterranean on my way to the south of France and Spain. I had already used this method of making quick money on my first trip to Brazil with Miguel.

The best way to find a pawn shop would be to ask someone who could point me in the right direction, and I decided to enter into a conversation with a transient who looked like he'd be well informed on the subject.

In my best Italian, I asked the man if he knew where I could pawn a few items. Without hesitation, he responded, "Ahh yes. *Il Monte Pieta.*" I couldn't believe it was named the same as in Uruguay… *El Monte Piedad.* He gave me the address and pointed me in the right direction. I had always thought the name originated from Italy, especially since there were many of us of Italian descent in Montevideo.

At the pawn shop, I was successful in getting a few more bills in my pocket. Feeling calmer about my immediate financial situation, I took the road southwest, trying to stay near the coast. The plan was to go to Genoa, visit Pisa and Florence, then head to Rome, the capital.

One night, under the dim light of a Florentine lantern, I took out my well-worn diary and began to jot down notes about my trip since Berne. Sometimes I enjoyed writing my accounts in verse, as I enjoyed reading and re-reading the Jose Hernandez classic, *Martin Fierro*, which had become like a bible to me during this journey.

*April 5, 1966*
   *It has been just a few days since I had traversed the Swiss Alps, enjoying the beautiful snow-capped vistas, trying to reach my ancestral country of origin. Finally reaching Italy, I felt exhilarated. This was something I had always dreamed about… to see where my ancestors*

*called home through my own eyes. Now, I can finally communicate in a familiar language, without having to resort to those appalling dictionaries.*

*I'll never forget Marello's face when I revved up my Indian's engine in front of his restaurant, testing his ear. Both he and I could always distinguish the type of motorcycle simply by its sound. It was great catching up with him, remembering our bike racing days in far away Montevideo.*

*April 7, 1966*
*I sent a telegram to my parents asking them to send money to the Bank of Rome. I'm already on my way to the capital.*

From Turin I turned toward Genoa, where I had the opportunity to visit many plazas and monuments. I was most impressed by Via Garibaldi, the main street in the historical center of Genoa, well known for its ancient and grand palaces. I also enjoyed visiting the port of Genoa, and I pondered if, in a city that gave birth to Christopher Columbus, there could be another sailor as bold and risky as he was.

On the streets of Genoa I met a Chilean man who had emigrated to Italy years earlier, and upon seeing a Uruguayan license plate on the rear of my Indian, just had to introduce himself to satisfy his curiosity.

"Hi, I'm Atilio," he said in Spanish.

"Hello. I'm Carlos," I answered.

"Are you coming from Montevideo?" he asked.

"Yes I am."

"Well then, let's have a drink! I am from Chile and would be delighted to share a few moments with a fellow South American!" he offered enthusiastically.

We went to a nearby bar and instantly hit it off. Atilio invited me to stay with him and his family for a few days. I, of course, could not decline his offer.

I followed Atilio on his small Vespa moped to his home. When he arrived, he introduced me to his family... and honestly, his 17 year old daughter's beauty left me absolutely speechless. I quickly collected myself and proceeded to join them for a wonderful dinner prepared by his wife.

Atilio's daughter Rosetta sat next to me at the dinner table and, in Italian, kept asking all about my trip. The entire dinner conversation was dedicated to the details of how I managed to travel so far on an old motorcycle. I shared many stories with this generous and hospitable family.

After dinner, Rosetta brazenly asked me if I could take her on a ride on my bike. I was taken aback at her forwardness, especially since she had asked me in front of her parents. Atilio must have noticed my surprised expression and quickly said it was ok if I wanted his daughter to show me around town. I accepted her invitation and off we went to explore the city.

"Are you enjoying spending time with me?" she asked.

"More than you know," I responded in Italian. "Do you understand my Italian?"

"Of course," she said in Spanish. "Wanna dance?"

"Dance? Sure, but just so you know, I have no money," I stated, trying to conserve every penny.

"Don't worry. My treat."

We ended the night with Rosetta becoming another part of my many adventures, but we did not sleep together. Frankly, though, her beauty had me thinking I would one day return to find her. Without a doubt, she would remain a strong memory for the rest of my trip.

I left Genoa and headed toward Pisa on a beautiful sunny morning. Before arriving, I stopped at a small field to setup my tent as it was starting to get dark. I figured I'd cruise through Pisa quickly and continue on to Florence, deviating a bit from the coastal route.

The next morning I left for Pisa and stopped at a service station to wash up and groom myself since I'd be visiting the popular Leaning Tower of Pisa. Once there, I took it all in and even toured around the adjoining areas of interest. I then decided to continue to Florence in search of more art.

Florence, famous for its museums and works of art, had been a goal of mine for a long time. The narrow streets and old ornate buildings gave the city an impressive artistic character.

To enter the Uffizi Gallery I had to buy a ticket. There was no way around that. This was an opportunity I could not pass up, however. I figured maybe I could make it up by eating one less plate of food, but it would be worth it seeing all those famous works of art housed inside one of the oldest and most famous art museums in the world.

As soon as I entered, I felt fulfilled. I was looking at what many rich people in the world have not seen. I didn't need money to appreciate the art that has been so admired throughout the ages. I thought of those art books I studied in Montevideo, of how involved I was in the art scene, and of what that overused word had meant to those who died for it. Art!

I enjoyed Florence more than any other city I had encountered on this journey. It's too bad that my financial situation did not allow me to stay longer than I did. I departed for Rome, where the money from my parents hopefully awaited.

I decided to ride inland instead of taking the coastal route so that I could see the towns of Arezzo and Perugia, two places recommended to me by many Italians. I knew I wouldn't be able to see everything, but I wanted to see as much as possible. Of course, I figured that after seeing Florence, the art capital of the world, nothing would compare. But I quickly realized I was wrong. Italian art was everywhere… spread out over the entire country. The works of Tintoretto, Michelangelo, Leonardo da Vinci, and many other famous artists, could be seen and enjoyed all over Italy.

Riding along the twisty roads, I reached Rome one sunny afternoon and immediately began exploring the wondrous city, full of history and art. The next day was the day I was supposed to meet Albert, the Danish motorcyclist I met thirty days ago, and promised to reconnect with in Rome at the Piazza del Popolo.

The first thing I did was find a campground where I could set up camp that was near the city. Once located, I pitched my tent, took a warm shower, and counted the little money I had left. The next morning I headed right to the bank to pick up the money my parents had sent me.

I quickly parked, then entered the large doors of the old building. Saying "old" is superfluous since modern construction was nowhere to be seen in this city.

It was not much later that I discovered that all the banks in Uruguay were on strike indefinitely, and no money was waiting for me. Now I was really stuck with little money and no easy way to get more in a reasonable amount of time.

The watch that Helena had given me in Mexico showed that I was running late for my meeting with Albert at 3pm at the Piazza del Popolo. I asked for directions, and my Indian began to cruise in and out of the Roman traffic, surprising people due to its sheer size and volume. Large motorcycles were not common in Europe yet from what I had noticed, so my Indian always called attention to itself.

I reached the Piazza del Popolo, making good time, and while sitting on my bike a man came up to me and asked how many cubic centimeters my engine was. I told him, and he turned and enthusiastically yelled, "Nino! Nino! Twelve-hundred! It's twelve-hundred!"

He couldn't believe that in the land of the Fiat 500 there could possibly be a motorcycle with more than double the engine size as the automobile.

While waiting for Albert, I wrote in my journal.

*April 10, 1966*
*I'm waiting for Albert, the Danish guy I met in Brussels. I'm here a little early for our arranged meeting, and I'm wondering if he'll show up. It is a bit unusual for two casual acquaintances who met a month earlier to find each other again after each of us has travelled three separate countries.*

Arriving right on time, Albert was happy to see me and my Indian again. He asked how I survived the snowy Alps. After trading stories about our last month's travels in Europe, Albert told me he has been living in his Chilean friend's aunt's house while she was away on vacation. He invited me to join him and his friend to spend some time in a proper house rather than in tents and campgrounds.

We left for the house and upon arriving I noticed it was more of a mansion where we could live like kings… at least for a little while. Albert introduced me to his friend Sergio after I parked my Indian in the huge garage.

After a couple of days of the good life, Sergio announced that his aunt was returning and we had to leave. Luckily,

Albert and I had met two girls… a Chilean and a Peruvian. They invited us to stay with them for a while.

They had no garage, so I had to park my bike on the street. I would stare at my mechanical companion many times from the balcony that faced the street. Albert's bike, being significantly smaller than mine, could fit in the apartment's hallway.

One morning, as had become my routine, I stepped out onto the balcony and stared down to the street to check on the Indian. To my utter shock and horror, she was gone. Stolen.  My heart was pounding from panic, anger, and sadness. I couldn't help but think that it had to be a group of thieves that had stolen it because it would take many men to be able to lift a bike of that size onto a truck. It would have been nearly impossible for them to start the bike since I had rigged it with three hidden electrical bridges that needed to be switched on before the starter would even work. It was my own anti-theft system, made specifically to prevent things like this from happening.

Confident in my modifications, I immediately went out looking for the bike in the nearby Roman neighborhoods. Sure enough, I found her not far from the apartment, abandoned on a side street. Needless to say, I was ecstatic that my little electrical tricks had done their job.

It was obvious they had dragged the motorcycle a few blocks with the intention of starting it and riding away. Since they could not figure out how to get it running, they gave up.

After this scare, I decided to return to a more secure campground. Before arriving I decided to stop at the bank again, but again left disappointed as the banks in Uruguay were still on strike.

*April 16, 1966*
*The Indian was stolen, and the feeling that I was at the end of my journey had me mortified until I managed to find it. Something as simple as the loss of my dear Indian did not figure into my plans.*

*When I found the bike abandoned on a street, I couldn't help but yell out, "Hello again, old friend!"*

*April 17, 1966*
*Money is still scarce, and I'm still waiting for $200 from Uruguay. I paid for a week at the campground and split the rest of my money seven ways so I would have something for each day of the week. I doubt the strike in Uruguay will last another week.*

*I have enough to buy myself a large piece of bacon, a long Italian baguette, and a bottle of cheap red wine each day. In the meantime, I'll keep exploring this wonderful city.*

The days passed, and I managed to split my food rations to two meals a day... I would cut the bacon into strips, make a delicious sandwich with the bread, and wash it all down with wine, which was surprisingly cheaper than water. The food was nothing to write home about, but the quality of my meals was not that important to me. Honestly, I was happy I could feed myself each day, but the best meals were truly the spirit of my voyage and the memories I was making on this adventure.

Albert and I would go exploring local points of interest, admiring the intricate architecture and taking in all the amazing works of art that seemed abundant in Rome.

One day Albert went out at night and I decided to stay in camp. I noticed that after many hours, he had not returned. I began to worry. The next morning, when he still had not returned, I desperately went to find Sergio and explained to him what was going on. We immediately went out to look at all the hospitals, police stations, and clinics in the area for fear that something had happened to our friend.

We found him at the hospital in the center of Rome. He had an accident on his bike the night before, but though the doctors said it wasn't serious, they kept him overnight for observation.

He suffered many scratches on his right leg and arm, and a small blow to the head. Albert told us he had met up with some guys the night before and they went drinking. A few too many was the cause for his loss of control on a curve. The motorcycle was fine except for a crooked handlebar, which could be easily fixed.

Albert left the hospital and we continued touring around Rome. We visited St. Peter's Basilica, the Vatican, and many other historical points of interest. I would stop every day at the bank to check on the money situation. Finally, the money arrived and I would be able to head north.

Albert and I said our goodbyes. The Indian and I were ready for our trek north, but this time taking an alternate route up the coast. The idea was to see as much as possible. I cruised through Civitavecchia, Piombino, and Livorno, then back through Pisa and Genoa before reaching the pawn shop in Turin to claim the items I had pawned. While in Turin, I decided to not bother Marello since he and his wife were so generous and attentive my first time around.

I had ridden past Genoa on my way to Turin, but the temptation to see Rosetta's beauty again had me reversing my tracks. I was with Atilio and his family again for two days and the romantic rides out with Rosetta continued.

When it came time for me to leave, Rosetta surprised me by giving me a kiss on the lips right in front of her parents.

The South of France, with its different class of tourism, was beckoning. In Nice, Toulon, and Marseilles one could smell the money of both the residents and the tourists. The contrast between this type of exploration and the kind my Indian and I were doing was striking. With very little gasoline for my bike, and even less food for me, we still pushed forward, taking it all in.

Finding cheap lodging was impossible, and I had no choice but to keep riding until I could find something more in line with my poor economic condition. I stopped several times to write in my journal, where I could express the emotions of the moment. Sometimes I'd write with a smile on my lips... sometimes with moisture in my eyes. But many times when I would start a sad note, it would end up transforming into a tale of euphoric joy.

*May 3, 1966*

*I watch the people leaving a luxurious hotel and I ask myself if I will ever get the opportunity to experience something like this... if I will ever sleep on a decent bed, take a hot shower, or eat a decent meal.*

*I don't want to give the impression that I am envious or angry at any of these people. I'm only thinking about how at this very moment, it's impossible for me to be where they are, but perhaps one day in the distant future I'll have the opportunity. For now, I have to be happy with sleeping on the beach, bathing in gas station bathrooms, and eating when I can.*

*Anyway, I consider myself lucky that I am able to be out here experiencing the world and appreciating the diverse cultures and their different ways of living. Fortunately, I am healthy enough to keep travelling in these dangerous conditions, and I do not for once regret setting out on this adventure that has given me so many experiences that would otherwise be very difficult to obtain.*

Rumbling west down the French coastline, I headed toward Spain. I finally crossed the border after a few days, and oriented myself toward Barcelona. I took a detour toward the beach and crossed into Badalona, where I discovered a beautiful yet reasonably priced campground on the edge of the Mediterranean. It was the perfect location to relax for a couple of days. I paid, set up my tent, unloaded my belongings, and went looking for a warm shower. However, staring at the ocean I couldn't resist taking a dip first.

The owners of the campground had a young dog that quickly became my friend. I've always loved animals, and this dog would be my companion during my entire stay in Badalona.

When I would sit on the beach to write in my journal, the dog would lay next to me awaiting my friendly pats on the head. When I'd get up and walk, the dog would chase me and nip at my heels playfully.

I enjoyed the peace and tranquility for two days. On the third day, I arrived in Barcelona. I walked the famous "Paseo de las Flores" admiring its amazing beauty. The best part was being able to communicate in my native language, something I hadn't been able to do in quite a while. Every time I would speak with someone, being able to communicate clearly was such a joy that I wouldn't want the conversation to end. This allowed me to make many friends in Spain, two of which rode mopeds and served as my local Barcelona tour guides. By night I would return to the beach in Badalona, and by day I'd reconnect with Luis and Jose and go to Barcelona, where all the action was.

On one of those day trips I met a tall, beautiful blonde named Maude. Though I had made several female friends on this adventure, this one was a little out of the ordinary with her Nordic looks and sculpted figure. She spoke very little Spanish so we communicated in English. Maude was a professional Dutch model working on Spanish TV. She was staying in a nice hotel and we became fast friends. At that point we became three... my Indian, Maude, and me... exploring all around the outskirts of Barcelona.

Luis and Jose would join us from time to time and they would criticize me for letting Maude pay for our meals. I told them that the Nordic culture was more progressive and women would commonly ask men out and pay themselves. Luis and Jose were nonetheless still bothered by it all and would argue about it with me to no end. Since Maude hardly spoke any Spanish, they would often discuss their thoughts right in front of her. When I'd translate what they were saying, her beautiful smile would accentuate the lack of importance she gave the whole subject.

One day I began planning to cross the Sahara desert, a trip that would take me from Spain, across the Strait of Gibraltar into Morocco, then down all of Africa into Cape Town. I was told that I would have to check with Moroccan officials so they could gauge the current conditions and make sure I was prepared to make the crossing. Apparently they needed to make sure I had a reasonable amount of water with me as well as extra gasoline for my Indian. An itinerary would then need to be filed. If I failed to check in at pre-determined checkpoints along the way, they would send people in Jeeps or helicopters to look for me. I knew this would be a difficult journey, but I wanted to reach Cape Town quickly so I could then make my way to Brazil, then back home to Uruguay.

Still in Spain, I was spending a lot of time with Maude, and one day she asked me if she could accompany me on the rest of my trip. I managed to steer the conversation in a different direction, never telling her yes or no. I definitely did not feel comfortable taking her on such a grueling and dangerous ride through the Sahara. I'd have to put off my answer until later.

The nights in Barcelona were magnificent. The temperature was perfect and the surroundings were straight out of a dream. One night, as I was returning to Badalona, I turned a corner in the road too quickly and noticed a large oil slick extending from the middle of the road all the way to the sidewalks. I sped through this corner almost every night, leaning into the curve, remembering my racing days.

Unfortunately, it was too late to slow down or avoid the oil slick. When the Indian's tires made contact with the viscous liquid, time slowed down as I fell on my right side, my knee scraping along the road as the bike weighed on top of me, still spinning. Finally coming to a stop, I noticed that my right knee, the same one I had hurt in my accident in Panama, was bleeding.

At the same time I could hear the sound of another motorcycle coming around the same corner. Limping, I ran to the middle of the road to warn the rider, but again I was too late. I watched as his motorcycle spun out and he fell just as I did. Luckily, his bike was much lighter than mine and he only suffered minor scrapes and cuts. The rider was a local, and together we made our way to a Red Cross station for help.

That night I arrived back in Badalona, more disappointed than tired. I was disappointed in the unexpected, with the lack of maintenance of the road that could have killed me, and with my lack of caution in this whole situation. I laid down on my sleeping bag and fell deeply asleep. The next day my knee was in severe pain and I had trouble walking. That afternoon I tried to kick start my bike, but the pain in my leg was too strong. I tried with my left leg and just didn't have the strength to get it started. Frustrated, I began to write.

*May 15, 1966*
*Last night's fall had me thinking that the end of my adventure is near. It left me disappointed, with a bitter taste in my mouth and a fresh wound on my knee.*

*I'm so tired that I don't even want to think, but the fact that my adventure is drawing to a close is painful. My knee injury is quite ugly, and I wonder if it would take me too long to recuperate to be able to make the trek through the Sahara. I know the voyage through the desert will be tough, and if I'm going to do it, I'll have to be fully prepared.*

*I guess I'll wait a few days and make a decision later.*

Still writing, a young man approached me and we began to talk. I convinced him to help me start the Indian. He did, and I was off to Barcelona.

Passing by the curve where I had fallen the night before, I noticed the oil had been completely cleaned up, as if nothing had ever happened.

Arriving in Barcelona, I didn't want to turn off my motorcycle for fear of not being able to start it up again. Luckily, I ran into Jose and Luis, so I shut off the bike knowing that either of them could help me get back on track later.

"Hey, man! What's with the funeral face?" asked Luis laughingly.

"I had a motorcycle accident," I said seriously.

"Oh… what happened?"

I explained to them both in detail what had occurred the night before as they stared in amazement.

Maude had returned to Holland for a few days and left me the key to her hotel room, where I took advantage of the comfortable bed and the fact that I didn't have to return to Badalona at night. In any case, I was concerned and I knew it wasn't because of my injury, or because Maude was gone, or because I had little money left. I was worried because I had to make some very important decisions… for my health, and for a beautiful woman who wanted to accompany me across the dangerous desert.

After a couple of days in the hotel, I started feeling better so I decided to head back to Badalona one night to pick up a few things. When I arrived at my tent I noticed that some of my clothes were strewn about. I shined my headlight in that direction, thinking that the dog had gotten into my things. When I opened the tent and looked inside, I was shocked to find that all my belongings were missing. I had been robbed.

I immediately went to the campsite's office to report the robbery when two Spanish policemen, officers of the Civil Guard, entered, asking if anyone was missing anything. My face hopeful, I listened as they explained that they had in custody two men who they caught crossing the train tracks carrying two small suitcases. Suspicious, the police called out to them and they began to run. A chase ensued, but the burglars were quickly surrounded. All this had just happened right before I had arrived back at my tent. I identified my belongings and was able to return to the tent with everything intact.

*May 20, 1966*

*I don't want to be responsible for another human being. I don't want on my conscience what could possibly occur. I don't even have the desire to be responsible for myself at this point.*

*Crossing the Sahara will not be possible in the physical condition I am in, and I certainly don't have enough money to wait until I'm better.*

*I will have to tell Maude that I have decided to end my journey now and that I need to find a way to get back home to Uruguay. I'm tired of fighting the unknown, of suffering from pain and hunger. Continuing this voyage is a ridiculous thought.*

*Hopefully I can find a job somewhere and make enough to find passage to anywhere in South America, where at least I'll be closer to home. Somehow I will find a way to end this adventure.*

I've always been a very positive and happy person, even during bad times. I've endured worse situations than this before with no complaints, but on this particular day, I was tired of travelling the world and just wanted to return home.

Since I could already speak a somewhat passable English, I started looking for a job in one of the many coastal restaurants where English speaking tourists were plentiful. When told how much the jobs paid, I did the math. I would have to work for three months straight, live in my tent, and spend very little money to be able to afford the passage back to South America. Europe undoubtedly did not offer the same kinds of opportunities as the United States, where a man could live comfortably and save some money on one job's wage.

Once a week I would visit the Uruguayan Consulate to pick up any mail that may have been waiting for me. The consul happened to be a friend of one of my cousins in Uruguay. I explained to him my current situation, and we discussed it over dinner.

He managed to arrange passage for me and my Indian on a ship from the Argentine Maritime Shipping Line, and all I had to pay for was the cost of boarding the motorcycle. I explained that I did not want to be repatriated, and he assured me that would not occur and that he would arrange for my ticket. It then hit me that I had finally decided to end my journey.

The consul told me he would let me know when I could pick up my ticket, and that I should start making preparations for boarding the Indian. This could take a while, but I wasn't in a great hurry… and I really had no choice regardless.

*May 28, 1966*
*Today I took a deep breath, armed myself with courage, and explained to Maude that I planned to return to Uruguay and end my trip. She accepted my decision, but was a little sad because she had already planned on adventuring with me through the Sahara.*

*She also understood that my knee was not in the best shape, and that she was probably not well equipped to help me if anything were to happen in the desert. The most important thing is that we're still friends.*

The ship was in port. In five days it would embark for South America, with a quick stop in Lisbon, which was fine with me since it would give me the opportunity to visit Portugal.

I found my way to the ship's office, paid for stowing the Indian, and made all the necessary arrangements for my trip. Everything was set, and in a few days I would bring my motorcycle to the port to get it stowed for passage. The entire voyage would last 22 days, including the Lisbon stop as well as another in Santos, Brazil.

I enjoyed my final days on the old continent, and met up with Jose and Luis almost every night. We would talk for hours, about politics and religion, stories of my adventure, and countries we have all visited in the past. I'll never forget these friends, but the time for me to return home had come.

The decision to return to Uruguay had already been made, and nothing was going to change my mind. Filled with nostalgia, I bade my Spanish friends, and Maude, goodbye. I knew that all of this was part of my adventure, and that I would likely never see Maude again. As a professional model, she would have to continue to exploit her beauty and charm in front of the cameras, and I would have to search for my future.

# 14.

# Returning Home

I embarked on the Argentine ship, headed for Lisbon, Santos, and Montevideo. A huge crane lifted the Indian as if it were a feather, and gently deposited it into the cargo hold, where it would stay until we reached Uruguay. I felt separation anxiety and realized how attached I had become to my mechanical companion. I knew I wouldn't see her for several days, but I was happy that I would get to take a well deserved rest from the road.

The next day the ship embarked to Portugal, amid several blasts of its horn. Upon reaching the port of Lisbon, the horns repeated themselves to announce our arrival. We would be there for a couple of days, and I planned to take advantage of that time to get to know the city that would be my last in the old continent.

*June 1, 1966*

*Today I arrived in Lisbon on the ship that would take me on a long voyage to Montevideo. They placed me in a cabin that I have to share with a man who I think is Spanish because of the type of beret he is wearing.*

*We greeted each other and would run into each other every so often and always at night since we shared a room.*

I enjoyed a day and a half in Lisbon, exploring the parts of the city nearest the port, and not much else due to my limited time and the fact that my knee was still bothering me. Before I knew it, we were on the open sea again, and I was a little sad we were leaving the coasts of Europe.

The days were long and restful, and I forgot what it felt like to be hungry as there was plenty of food. I made a small group of friends on the ship and we would get together and play card games to pass the time. Among my new friends was a history professor from Argentina, a German named Rolf, and two other guys travelling together.

The days at sea were long and boring. To me, this was a time of reflection, of memories, rest, and recovery from my time on the road. My new friends were curious about my trip and listened intently as I told my stories. Rolf was particularly interested since he was planning on hitchhiking through South America on an adventure of his own.

I proudly showed pictures and newspaper clippings from all over the world. Every one of the 26 countries I had visited had left me with memories, both good and bad, but strong enough to endure for the rest of my life.

One of the games we played to pass the time was a word game where we'd have to name something that started with a particular letter. When the subject was cities, I had a huge advantage having just travelled the world, and my friends had to borrow an atlas from the ship's library to verify the city names I would come up with.

I kept wondering what my future would be once I returned home. I had so many thoughts in my head that it was difficult to sort through them all. Would I be able to start a company and be successful? Could I use what I had learned on my trip in my own country? I knew that I learned a lot during those two years, and I wondered if I would be able to apply that knowledge somehow.

I tried to imagine the city that I left almost two years prior, and I could not wait to see its borders once again.

*June 14, 1966*
*Today we crossed the equator. To celebrate, crew members sorted through passengers looking for anyone who wanted to sing or could play an instrument.*

When they came to our cabin asking if we wanted to participate in the celebration, both me and my cabin mate Jerome declined.

After they left, I commented to Jerome that I used to play the "bandoneon", an accordion-like instrument, as a child, but that I highly doubted there was one on board, or that I would even remember how to play anything after 13 years of not picking one up.

Jerome looked at me incredulously, and said, "My name is Jerome Baires, the first bandoneon player to Francisco Canaro, and I'm returning from concerts in Asia and Europe. There... below the bunk... " he pointed. "There are two instruments."

I picked one up and laid it on my lap and immediately began playing "La Cumparsita" as if it was 13 years ago. Jerome picked up the other bandoneon and joined me.

The series of coincidences for this to occur are mesmerizing... sharing a room with a famous musician who happened to have two bandoneons with him, picking one up like time had never passed, playing together on an Argentine ship where musicians were being sought to join in the celebration of crossing the equator.

The knocking on our cabin door broke our concentration. The sound of melodic Argentine tangos gave us away, and we were led to join the party. Jerome and I played a duet that pleased even the most demanding critics, not due to my skills, but rather Jerome's amazing talent that proved he was a true master of the music loved by so many on the shores of the La Plata River.

Jerome and I became famous on that small ship.

We pulled into port in Santos, Brazil. In a few short days I would be back in Montevideo, the final destination on my long voyage.

I stared at the Brazilian coastline from the deck of the ship and I began to think about Manuel. What has become of him? Is he ok? Did he make it back to Brazil after all the trouble in the United States? Will I ever see him again?

More questions began pouring into my mind. How will my parents react when I get home? Would my girlfriend from so long ago still be there? What about my friends?

Predicting that Uruguayan customs inspectors haven't changed, I gave Rolf a camera and tape recorder I picked up in the United States, the same ones I had pawned in Italy. I didn't want any hassles from the customs inspectors, and since Rolf was just passing through, they were less likely to take anything from him.

One day prior to arriving in Montevideo, I sat on the deck and began to write.

*June 23, 1966*
*I will finally be back home. After 22 days at sea, resting and eating, my knee is healed and I can't wait to see my family.*

It was a sad, grey, cloudy day when we arrived in Montevideo. From aboard the ship I observed a land that seemed foreign. After two years and 26 countries, I saw Uruguay as just one more. Montevideo looked smaller than I remembered, seeing it through eyes now accustomed to more impressive skylines.

While docking in the port of Montevideo, I saw my journalist friends from TV Channel 12 and I was a bit embarrassed by the whole thing.

I waited for the Indian to be unloaded, and when I saw her I felt whole again. She had been my faithful companion for two years, and it had been 22 days since I last laid eyes on her.

I had to go through customs, where they checked my baggage. After getting all the papers in order to claim my Indian, I left customs to meet up with my family and friends.

My parents cried tears of joy, and also of sadness at seeing their road-weary and much thinner son. My old girlfriend Nibia was also there and she ran up and planted a big kiss on me.

After many hugs and greetings that showed the love of those who missed me, I got on my bike, started her up, and led a large caravan of friends and family back to my house.

It was unbelievable to me that I was again riding along the cobbled streets in the old city by the port on my way to my old house. My passenger was Rolf, who had planned to stay a couple of days in Montevideo.

We arrived at home. I parked the Indian in front of the same door we had departed from two years earlier, and we all entered the house to enjoy a grand luncheon prepared by my mother.

The next day, under a radiant sun, Rolf and I headed to the city center. We took the coastal route, which brought back many memories. It had only been two years since I left, but it seemed like much longer. Everything looked strange to me, smaller. In my final entry in my journal, I described my return to Montevideo a few days earlier.

*June 23, 1966*

*I arrived in Montevideo. It's sad, overcast, and grey outside. From a distance I can see the Salvo Palace, and it looks tiny. The buildings on the skyline seem very short and unimpressive. These two years of adventure have apparently warped my memories of this place.*

*When we disembarked from the ship, I gave Rolf my camera and tape recorder to sneak through customs. As Rolf passed through, an inspector tried to confiscate my items. Since he could not speak Spanish, I acted as his translator and helped defend his position, as well as my belongings. They finally let him through.*

*With my last remaining money, I had purchased four bottles of liquor on the ship. The customs inspector, already mad at me for defending Rolf, told me I could only bring two bottles. I immediately opened two bottles and poured their contents into a garbage can, then handed the agent the empty bottles. He looked at me dumbfounded.*

*When I tried to get the Indian, another customs inspector said they could not release it because the person in charge of signing the paperwork was not present. I simply told them that if the person required to get this done didn't show up soon, I would talk about it on TV that night. My threat worked, and fifteen minutes later, I had my motorcycle back.*

*I got the feeling that everything was starting off badly in my own country, which made me very sad.*

On Wednesday, Rolf wanted to go to the central post office to send letters to Germany. I invited him for pizza at my favorite local pizza place. When we arrived, I parked the Indian, and as we began walking we noticed people staring at us. Both Rolf and I were wearing sandals and shorts, which was apparently uncommon in this area. I actually felt uncomfortable in my own home country.

On Thursday, I took Rolf to the border of Montevideo as he planned to continue north. We said our goodbyes with a heartfelt hug and I wished him well on his own adventure. I then turned around and rode back home as it was starting to get dark.

The weekend arrived and I planned to take a short trip to Punta del Este. I was starting to feel the hunger for the road again, and these quick jaunts afforded me the time to reminisce about my adventurous journey.

I reached Solymar when a policeman, also on a motorcycle, pulled me over for riding with a large box attached to the rear fender. I couldn't believe what I was hearing. I felt like telling him to fuck off, but instead I proceeded to tell him that my Indian, that box, and I had travelled 26 countries over two continents, and during the entire two years of that trip, not a single person had told us that we weren't allowed to ride with a box attached to the rear fender. I showed him my stamp-filled passport, along with my journal filled with foreign newspaper clippings about my voyage. The cop, red with embarrassment, let me go.

From my journey, I brought with me a suitcase full of dreams and ideas that began to clash against the forced smiles of the Uruguayans. I had learned new technologies that could be applied in this country, but I needed someone with vision and a desire to invest in my ideas so that I could capitalize on them. Unfortunately, I was constantly met with negativity and a "we can't do that here" mentality. I thought back longingly at the American way of life, where change and innovation was embraced, and I realized that this attitude was also my own.

I had demonstrated this when I invented the water heater before I embarked on my two-year trek, and in the short time I had worked in the United States. The Americans had promised me a job, paid studies, and the arrangement of my immigration papers if I ever decided to return.

I liked my country, but this experience had matured me in many ways. I've always been a dreamer, but one that strived to make those dreams come true. Case in point, this entire trip was undertaken solely to explore what existed beyond these small borders. No one could ever convince me to not follow my dreams, and I would not rest until they were fulfilled. Something inside would push me, no matter the sacrifice. I was born this way, and I will die this way.

Not even a month had passed when I made the decision to return to the United States. I explained to my friends and family that in America they believed in my ideas and would provide the nurturing environment to help develop these ideas into reality. I knew I would have to adapt to a new way of life and that I would miss many things from my country, but I saw no way to realize my dreams if I stayed in Uruguay.

I was so attached to my Indian that it was very difficult to come to the decision to sell it to pay for my trip north. One day I said goodbye to everyone, and also to my faithful companion that had accompanied me on such an important life's journey. Filled with emotion, I thought about what this machine would say to me if she could talk. I wrote these words…

*It's me, your motorcycle,*
*my skinny friend, old vagabond.*
*Showing you the world,*
*many countries, and beyond.*

*I'm the one that you bought,*
*with money tucked away.*
*The one that shared with you,*
*wild Bohemian days.*

*I'm the one at your side,*
*on those cold rainy nights.*
*Watching you sleep,*
*waiting for light.*

*The journey then ends,*
*coming home, winding down.*
*How we've grown side by side,*
*mile by mile, town by town!*

*And now marching north,*
*American dream in your sights.*
*No more room for old friends,*
*cast aside, price was right.*

*From your hands to a stranger's,*
*his chest puffed with pride.*
*But I'm sorry old friend,*
*I miss your touch when we ride!*

*And there will be others,*
*that last many more years.*
*My mechanics are faulty,*
*but I can still shed a tear.*

*In your mind I'm a memory,*
*of mad, crazy years.*
*Of wishing and dreaming,*
*of knowing no fear!*

*We peel back the memories,*
*both happy and sad.*
*The struggles… successes…*
*all the times that we had!*

*I speak to you now,*
*because of what we have shared.*
*Now I'm old, past my prime,*
*but my soul I have bared.*

*It's me, your motorcycle,*
*my skinny friend, old vagabond.*
*Let's meet up again and go further beyond!*

*- Your Indian Chief*

Memories flooded my brain like a whirlwind while I rode along the old streets I left behind years ago in search of new horizons. This journey with my old motorcycle had been the springboard which gave me the momentum to emigrate. I had discovered a world so different than mine that upon my return I could not find what I was looking for… someone that believed in what I had learned and wanted to help make changes for the better. That someone did not exist in my country.

I believed that human beings were inhabitants of the world, not just one country, but so many people didn't even have the basic necessities of life. If I didn't leave then, I probably would never be able to.

It was appalling to see what was happening in my country. There were people who made a living scavenging through garbage cans looking to sell what could be recycled, and even to eat from the garbage. Even after decades, the government has done nothing to alleviate the ever growing problems.

I recognized this careless attitude from my travels through South and Central America, where people were simply cast aside, resigned to their fate. My trip taught me to appreciate diversity and change, and to base life changing decisions on my own belief system. I could measure the poverty in the Andes against the poverty in other countries, but in the end, it's all poverty.

These same roads were travelled by Che Guevara in the early 1950's. I saw the same injustices that he did, and understood his desire to try to improve things. His path followed an ill-fated idealism... a very different methodology than mine.

What he failed to see was that the goal should be to try to create opportunities that would raise the middle class by creating jobs. I had seen 26 countries on my trip, and after emigrating I saw seven more travelling for work. It's no wonder my way of thinking was so different than that of a man who never left his cocoon, regardless of sharing the same basic humanitarian values.

How different would things have turned out had I been born in the cradle of luxury? I probably would not have laid the tracks that took me from adventurer and vagabond, to a serious family man... or go from blue collar worker to the vice president of a multinational corporation.

I had experienced every class... had lived with simple natives as well as the wealthy. I was convinced my experience mattered. I knew that opportunities could help a town progress and grow. I had seen it all over the world, and

I couldn't believe that everyone didn't simply copy the political system that led to advancement and progress.

I couldn't understand bureaucracies or the lack of honesty and compassion from the government. I couldn't believe that it hurt me more to see a hungry child than it did them.

# 15.

# Reunion

After many years, I wrote a letter to Manuel.

*Dear friend,*

*I hope you forgive me for not writing you until now, but I just want you to know that I have never forgotten you.*

*After we separated in the United States, I continued travelling and explored most of Europe with little trouble. Good roads, old and interesting cities, and one or two exciting adventures, like always. Although I enjoyed myself, I deeply missed your companionship.*

*In Spain, when I was planning to head out to Africa, I hit an oil slick on a curve and reopened the wounds on my leg. I decided then to end my adventure and took advantage of free passage on a ship bound for Uruguay.*

*The ship made a quick stop in Brazil, but we were not allowed to disembark, making it impossible for me to try to contact you at that time.*

*I arrived in Montevideo and it seemed so small and disorganized to me that I lost all desire to stay. After 40 days I sold my Indian and bought a plane ticket to the United States. They rehired me at the company where we used to work, and I am quickly climbing the ranks.*

*Now, you better sit down for what I am about to tell you next. In New York, I met a woman and got married. Yes, you heard correctly... I am married and very happy! Of course, that doesn't mean I've lost the desire to keep exploring. I'm already thinking about buying a new motorcycle.*

*You have no idea how much I want to see you again and reminisce about the past, both the suffering and the joy that we shared like brothers.*

*I have no idea if this letter will ever reach you since I don't quite remember your address very well. If you do get this, please keep in touch. I hope you remember Spanish well enough to be able to read this.*

*Awaiting your response eagerly, I say goodbye to you with a big hug.*

*Your friend always,*
*El Flaco.*

Apparently, Manuel never received this letter.

In 1986, I took my family on a vacation to Rio de Janeiro and Brasilia. I had a very important ulterior motive for this trip… I wanted to find my old friend. As soon as we arrived at the hotel on the beach in Leblon, I looked through the local phone book searching for the friend I lost contact with so many years ago in the United States.

"Manuel Capelo"… there was one listed in the town of Cascadura, where I had first met Manuel and where our journey had started. I nervously dialed the number. The voice of an elderly man answered. I asked if he was Manuel Capelo Filho (junior). He said no, but that his son lived in the house behind his. I left him the hotel's phone number with a message to contact me.

After about one hour, the phone rang.

"Hello?" I answered.
"Hello," he responded.
"Who is this?" I asked.

"Flaco? Is that you?" Manuel asked, his voice trembling.

"Yes, it's me... and I want to see you."

"I can't believe you're here!"

"Yes, I am here! Let's get together as soon as possible!"

I gave him the hotel's address and he told me he would be here around four in the afternoon. At 3:30 I was already in the hotel lobby waiting for him. Suddenly, he entered the building and we saw each other from afar. We greeted each other from a distance with exaggerated arm movements, as if that would bring us closer together faster. Then we hugged just like we did on that day in New York, and began asking each other all sorts of questions. We had so much catching up to do that time passed without us even realizing it. Manuel had five kids, worked as a police officer in a prison in Rio, and had heart problems.

I invited him to dinner with my family, and after we paid the bill, Manuel mentioned that the amount we paid for that one meal could feed his family for a month.

The next day Manuel invited us to his house to meet his wife and children and to continue catching up with everything that had happened to us in the last twenty years.

He lived modestly in a small house built in his father's backyard, and it was obvious that supporting a family of five on a policeman's salary was not an easy thing. Before we left, we gave each of his children a ten dollar bill, and his wife quickly gathered the bills to keep in a safer place.

Manuel continued writing music for samba schools and invited us to one of their rehearsals in the neighborhood of Santa Isabel. My family got to meet the poor but happy people that gladly spent any bit of money they had on their costumes for the famous *Carnaval* of Rio. It was their way to celebrate their happiness, through song and dance, and gave them the motivation to keep working hard and saving for the next year's festivities. It was a way of life that was very different from what we were used to in the United States.

After spending a week in Rio we travelled to Brasilia, but not before saying our goodbyes to Manuel and his beautiful family, and with the promise of keeping in touch and hopefully meeting again on any future trips to the southern continent.

Epilogue

I had to reach old age to realize that happiness, well-being, and progress have to be found on your own. Being happy in life is accomplished by doing what you like to do, and the rest will follow. Life is fleeting and one has to embrace it and attack it with optimism. Things won't just fall from the sky... you have to work to achieve what you want regardless of the efforts. Every action has a consequence.

Surely, my mother's strong character and the strict rules of the Catholic schools in my youth persuaded me to break free of such demanding and regulated environments. Genetics could also have played a part in my adventurous nature. My great grandfather boarded his entire family on a boat bound to a country where they did not speak the language, in search of a better life, and that effort paid off.

Every human being has opportunity in his hands, and it's simply waiting to be taken. We are inhabitants of Earth and have the ability to adapt to living in even the harshest conditions. We cannot create artificial limitations that halt our true path and force us to live a life we don't want to live. Each of us is a unique individual, with unique talents and desires, among the billions of inhabitants on this planet.

During my life I have often been criticized for making snap decisions. Doing things without extensive analysis has always been a part of who I am. I believe there is nothing worse than indecision and that it is often better to act than to stagnate. That trait is what offered me the opportunity to know the world, experience other cultures, other ways of thinking, and above all, to learn that nothing is impossible with enough effort, and failure is nothing more than a learning opportunity.

The resolutions we make at any given time will undoubtedly change our future. It is these mental impulses that push us to reach our goals and fulfill our dreams. No one has the right to take away our freedom to dream.

I had to walk long and far to realize that those fancy tourists on the French Riviera were not enjoying themselves more than I was, travelling on my old motorcycle with little money. I learned that life is what we make of it, and money does not provide happiness, it simply provides comfort. These two things can easily be separated. We can be rich and unhappy, or poor and happy.

What's important is that we enjoy every moment we have right now, since these moments are fleeting, and they will mean nothing once the time arrives to leave this Earth. Life will occasionally give us a wakeup call so that we realize that advantage must be taken of every opportunity that is offered.

We, as humans, often take for granted the little things in life that surround us every day because they are either too close to us to notice, or they are too easily obtained. A blooming flower, a full moon, twinkling stars at night, a calm or enraged sea, the horizon... that distant horizon we continue to watch from the tracks we have laid in our lifetimes... a symbol that there is always something more... hopes... dreams... just beyond our reach.

# About the author

Carlos Caggiani was born in Montevideo, Uruguay in 1940. In 1966, he emigrated to the United States where he studied and worked in engineering.

He obtained several patents for medical products, aviation and industrial turbines, retiring in 2002 as the vice president of a multinational corporation.

In 1998 he wrote *Deshojando Recuerdos*, a book of poems in Spanish about his childhood. In 2000, he wrote *El Nuevo Martín Fierro*, a compilation of poems about his adventurous two year motorcycle trip.

His Spanish language *Huellas y Horizontes*, written in 2009, is a more detailed history of his amazing journey around the world on his 1947 Indian Chief motorcycle.

The English version, *Tracks and Horizons*, is a faithful translation completed in 2010 by his son Ed, working in conjunction with Carlos to ensure not only the accuracy of the events, but the tone and emotion of his original Spanish telling.

Made in the USA
Lexington, KY
27 September 2011